Other Books and Series by Jeff Bowen

Compilation of History of the Cherokee Indians and Early History of the Cherokees by Emmet Starr with Combined Full Name Index (Hardbound & Softbound)

1901-1907 Native American Census Seneca, Eastern Shawnee, Miami, Modoc, Ottawa, Peoria, Quapaw, and Wyandotte Indians (Under Seneca School, Indian Territory)

1932 Census of The Standing Rock Sioux Reservation with Births and Deaths 1924-1932

Kiowa, Comanche, Apache, Fort Sill Apache, Wichita, Caddo and Delaware Indians Birth and Death Rolls 1924-1932

Census of The Blackfeet, Montana, 1897- 1901 Expanded Edition

Eastern Cherokee by Blood, 1906-1910, Volumes I thru *XIII*

Choctaw of Mississippi Indian Census 1929-1932 with Births and Deaths 1924-1931 Volume I
Choctaw of Mississippi Indian Census 1933, 1934 & 1937, Supplemental Rolls to 1934 & 1935 with Births and Deaths 1932-1938, and Marriages 1936-1938 Volume II

Eastern Cherokee Census Cherokee, North Carolina 1930-1939 Census 1930-1931 with Births And Deaths 1924-1931 Taken By Agent L. W. Page Volume I
Eastern Cherokee Census Cherokee, North Carolina 1930-1939 Census 1932-1933 with Births And Deaths 1930-1932 Taken By Agent R. L. Spalsbury Volume II
Eastern Cherokee Census Cherokee, North Carolina 1930-1939 Census 1934-1937 with Births and Deaths 1925-1938 and Marriages 1936 & 1938 Taken by Agents R. L. Spalsbury And Harold W. Foght Volume III

Seminole of Florida Indian Census, 1930-1940 with Birth and Death Records, 1930-1938

Starr Roll 1894 (Cherokee Payment Rolls) Districts: Canadian, Cooweescoowee, and Delaware Volume One
Starr Roll 1894 (Cherokee Payment Rolls) Districts: Flint, Going Snake, and Illinois Volume Two
Starr Roll 1894 (Cherokee Payment Rolls) Districts: Saline, Sequoyah, and Tahlequah; Including Orphan Roll Volume Three

Cherokee Intruder Cases Dockets of Hearings 1901-1909 Volumes I & II

Indian Wills, 1911-1921 Records of the Bureau of Indian Affairs Books One thru *Seven*
Native American Wills & Probate Records 1911-1921
Turtle Mountain Reservation Chippewa Indians 1932 Census with Births & Deaths, 1924-1932

Other Books and Series by Jeff Bowen

Chickasaw By Blood Enrollment Cards 1898-1914 Volume I thru *V*

Cherokee Descendants East An Index to the Guion Miller Applications Volume I
Cherokee Descendants West An Index to the Guion Miller Applications Volume II
(A-M)
Cherokee Descendants West An Index to the Guion Miller Applications Volume III
(N-Z)

Applications for Enrollment of Seminole Newborn Freedmen, Act of 1905

Eastern Cherokee Census, Cherokee, North Carolina, 1915-1922, Taken by Agent
James E. Henderson   Volume I (1915-1916)
*   Volume II (1917-1918)*
*   Volume III (1919-1920)*
*   Volume IV (1921-1922)*

Eastern Cherokee Census, Cherokee, North Carolina, 1923-1929, Taken by Agent
James E. Henderson   Volume I (1923-1924)
*   Volume II (1925-1926)*
*   Volume III (1927-1929)*

Complete Delaware Roll of 1898

Applications for Enrollment of Seminole Newborn Act of 1905 Volumes I & II

North Carolina Eastern Cherokee Indian Census 1898-1899, 1904, 1906, 1909-
1912, 1914   Revised and Expanded Edition

1932 Hopi and Navajo Native American Census with Birth & Death Rolls (1925-
1931) Volume 1 - Hopi
1932 Hopi and Navajo Native American Census with Birth & Death Rolls (1930-
1932) Volume 2 - Navajo

Western Navajo Reservation Navajo, Hopi and Paiute 1933 Census with Birth &
Death Rolls 1925-1933

Cherokee Citizenship Commission Dockets 1880-1884 and 1887-1889
Volumes I thru *V*

Applications for Enrollment of Chickasaw Newborn Act of 1905
Volumes I thru *VII*
Cherokee Intermarried White 1906 Volume I thru *X*

Applications for Enrollment of Creek Newborn Act of 1905
Volumes I thru *XIV*
Applications for Enrollment of Choctaw Newborn Act of 1905 Volumes I thru *XX*

Choctaw By Blood Enrollment Cards 1898-1914 Volumes I thru *XX*

Other Books and Series by Jeff Bowen

Oglala Sioux Indians Pine Ridge Reservation 1932 Census Book I
Oglala Sioux Indians Pine Ridge Reservation Birth and Death Rolls 1924-1932
Book II

Census of the Sioux and Cheyenne Indians of Pine Ridge Agency
1896 - 1897 Book I
Census of the Sioux and Cheyenne Indians of Pine Ridge Agency
1898 - 1899 Book II

Northern Cheyenne Tongue River, Montana 1904 - 1932 Census
1904-1916 Volume I
Northern Cheyenne Tongue River, Montana 1904 - 1932 Census
1917-1926 Volume II
Northern Cheyenne Tongue River, Montana 1904 - 1932 Census
1927-1932 Volume III

Sac & Fox - Shawnee Estates 1885-1910 (Under Sac & Fox Agency)
Volumes I-VIII
Sac & Fox - Shawnee Estates 1920-1924 (Under The Sac & Fox Agency,
Oklahoma) & Wills 1889-1924 Volume IX
Sac & Fox - Shawnee Deaths, Cemetery, Births, & Marriage Cards (Under The Sac
& Fox Agency, Oklahoma) 1853-1933 Volume X
Sac & Fox - Shawnee Marriages, Divorces, Estates Log Books Volumes 1 & 2, Log
Book Births & Deaths (Under Sac & Fox Agency, Oklahoma)1846-1924 Volume XI
Sac & Fox - Shawnee Guardianships Part 1 (Under Sac & Fox Agency, Oklahoma)
1892-1909 Volume XII
Sac & Fox - Shawnee Guardianships, Part 2 (Under The Sac & Fox Agency,
Oklahoma) 1902-1910 Volume XIII
Sac & Fox - Shawnee Guardianships, Part 3 (Under The Sac & Fox Agency,
Oklahoma) 1906-1914 Volume XIV

Census of the Pima, Tohono O'odham (Papago), and Maricopa Indians of the Gila
River, Ak Chin & Gila Bend Reservations 1932 with Birth and Death Rolls 1924-
1932

Identified Mississippi Choctaw Enrollment Cards 1902-1909 Volumes I, II, III
Identified Mississippi Choctaw Enrollment Cards' Dawes Packets 1902-1909
Volumes IV, V & VI

Census of the Northern Navajo, Navajo Reservation, New Mexico, 1930 Volume I
Census of the Northern Navajo, Navajo Reservation, New Mexico, 1931 Volume II

Crow Agency Montana 1898-1905 Census Volume I 1898-1901 with Illustrations

Visit our website at **www.nativestudy.com** to learn more about these
other books and series by Jeff Bowen

TEXAS CHEROKEES
1820-1839
WITH
A DOCUMENT FOR LITIGATION
1921

SUBMITTED BY

GEORGE W. FIELDS, LAWYER
OKLAHOMA CITY, OKLAHOMA

COMPILED & TRANSCRIBED BY

JEFF BOWEN

NATIVE STUDY
Gallipolis, Ohio
USA

Originally published:
Santa Maria, California
2018

Reprinted by:

Native Study LLC
Gallipolis, OH
www.nativestudy.com

Library of Congress Control Number: 2022904252

ISBN: 978-1-64968-131-7

Made in the United States of America.

This book is dedicated to the Texas Cherokee who fought the good fight. Like any human being they wanted justice and fairness. They just wanted a place they could call home....

Table of Contents

Cherokee Boundaries Map   vi

Introduction   vii

The Texas Cherokees 1820 – 39   3

APPENDIX 1   65

APPENDIX 2   76

APPENDIX 3   93

APPENDIX 4   109

Drawing of Chief Bowles   111

Index   113

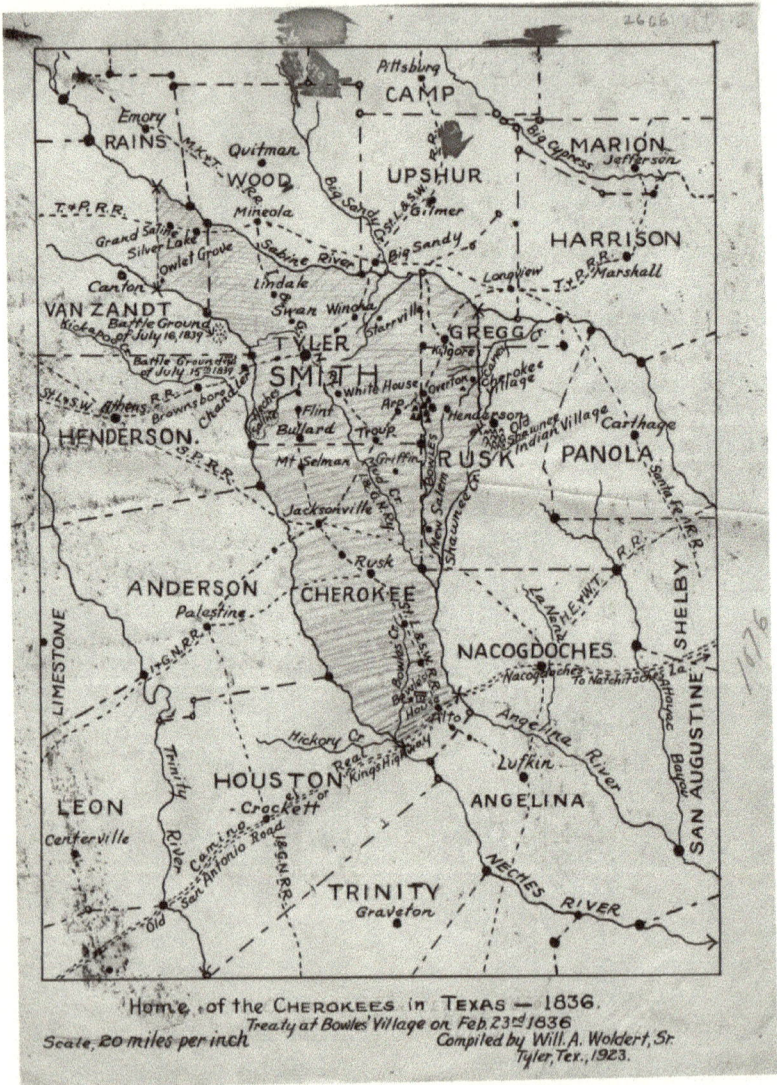

Home of the CHEROKEES in TEXAS — 1836.
Treaty at Bowles' Village on Feb. 23rd 1836
Scale: 20 miles per inch   Compiled by Will. A. Woldert, Sr.
                                  Tyler, Tex., 1923.

Will A. Woldert, Sr. Collection, #82.288 Box 1 folder 1, Manuscript Division, Oklahoma Historical Society Research Center, Oklahoma City, Oklahoma.

INTRODUCTION

George W. Fields, Jr., was a lawyer practicing in Oklahoma City, Oklahoma. He was the grandson of Chief Richard Fields one of the main leaders of the Texas Cherokee.

The heirs of the Texas Cherokee hired George W. Fields Jr., during their first organizational meeting in Oklahoma City, Oklahoma, on February 14, 1920. He filed a petition in the U.S. Supreme Court to sue the State of Texas in representation of those heirs, and it was denied.

In this book you will find the Cherokee applications of both George W. Fields and George Fields, Jr., showing the family connection to the original Texas Cherokee Chief Richard Fields. This is so you can understand the passion behind the document and realize that the attorney for the case had a vested interest in what happened a hundred years previous. Also, there is a copy of a letter and its envelope from 1930 where George W. Fields communicated with a Cherokee historian named Penelope Allen, showing that he had an interest in his family history and genealogy, and a desire to trace his family's origins. He was searching out from where his grandfather had descended.

There are two main characters in this true and tragic story. Both from similar backgrounds with mixed Scottish and Cherokee bloodlines. One of them, Chief Bowl, was born in North Carolina about 1756 and succeeded to the famous Chickamauga Cherokee Chief Dragging Canoe.[1] Chief John Bowles description at that time was, "an auburn haired, blue eyed half blood Scottish Cherokee about thirty-two years old."[2] The other, Richard Fields with a powerful description by two Moravian Missionaries, Steiner and De Shweinitz mentioned Fields as an interpreter for a Major Lewis, agent to the Cherokees in 1799. They said, "Dick Fields, a half-breed, clothed entirely in Indian fashion, with hunting-pouch girdle, etc., set with corals. This one seems to be a sensible and modest man, speaks a pure English, and receives an annual salary of three hundred dollars from the United States, as interpreter." They also stated, "Mr. Fields had a rifled gun with silver mountings and the finest trimmings on the stock, the work done by an artist in the State of Tennessee..."[3]   Both men had the same love for their people, both were manipulated by the Mexican Government and politicians as well as the white men fighting for the same rich Southeast Texas lands the Cherokee had settled first. It isn't that Chiefs Fields and Bowles couldn't hold their own against the evil process they were about to go through, they could. They were courageous and smart enough to handle it at first, it's that they, as the Cherokee have always been, were outnumbered by others who were totally lacking in integrity.

---

[1] Clarke, *Chief Bowles and the Texas Cherokees*, 7-8.

[2] Starr, *History of the Cherokee Indians*, 35.

[3] Allen, *History of the Cherokee Indians*, 512.

The Texas Cherokee under Chief Bowles and Chief Richard Fields first migrated to Texas around the year 1819. After a brief stay in Arkansas they moved south into the vicinity of present-day Dallas, Texas, which was then part of New Spain. They were there but a short time, only to be forced out by the wild tribes of the area and move further south stopping near Nacogdoches, Texas. Bowles and Fields requested permission to settle from the Spanish first, then approximately a year later sought permission from the Provisional Government of Mexico, then the Government of Mexico (stemming from both the Mexican War of Independence and the overthrow of Mexico's first emperor). Subsequently the Cherokee would renegotiate permission from both the Provisional Government of the Republic of Texas, and the Republic of Texas.

Needless to say each Government wanted the Cherokee for the advantage of power against the other. They all relied upon the Cherokees. The Cherokee warriors were known as sharpshooters, their rifles brought power. They wanted this peace loving yet powerful people to also serve as a buffer or wall between the wild Indian tribes in Texas. Each government, with its politicians, had motives, both public and private. No matter what the Cherokee did they were caught between what so many have termed as "two fires". They were going to be burned by these governments and all of them knew it. The only ones to show good faith with the slightest bit of trust were the Native Americans. Their word was their only assurance of being able to find a place and being accepted. They just never found anyone with power who wasn't a tyrant, except probably Sam Houston and a few others.

Unfortunately, the land the Cherokees lived on was coveted by others. At the very moment they were signing the treaty shown within these pages, deeds were being granted to white settlers, surveyors were mapping out property lines--all of this authorized by the same Provisional Government of the Republic of Texas that had insisted on a treaty to make sure the Cherokee either fought on their side or at least, not fight with their enemy the Mexican Government. Since that time to the present there hasn't been a single court of authority that has had the scruples to do the right thing by the descendants of a people that just wanted to plant their crops, educate their children, and live what we today call the American Dream.

The letter and envelope dated March 22, 1930, from Fields to Penelope Allen as well as the original history and arguments of Attorney George W. Fields that are transcribed within these pages were graciously given to me by a wonderful Western Cherokee historian and genealogist approximately nine years ago along with these few lines, "I've had these pages for almost forty years now. While I was at a genealogical society meeting I met this man who was the son-in-law of George W. Fields, Jr. After he had realized who I was and the Cherokee genealogical work I had done, and learning our offices were close by, he one day brought to me this Xerox copy of his father's-in-law history and arguments thinking I might do something with them." Dorothy Tincup Mauldin never did organize a compilation for this important piece of Cherokee history but honored this author with the task. The completion of this transcription today was helped because of the technology of the Internet, which gave me the ability to research archives, purchase old reference materials, and communicate with others--actions that years ago wouldn't have been within my reach.

Jeff Bowen
Gallipolis, Ohio
NativeStudy.com

[Copy of George Fields, Sr.'s Dawes Enrollment Card No. 4095]

TEXAS CHEROKEES

1820 – 1839

By Geo. W. Fields
Oklahoma City,
Oklahoma

1 9 2 1

THE TEXAS CHEROKEES

1820 – 39.

By the year of 1812, about one-fourth of the Cherokee Nation east had emigrated to the Arkansas Territory between the Arkansas and White Rivers. John Bowles, a chief, and a large number from Running Water Town, on the Mussel Shoals of the Tennessee, had left in the year 1794 and emigrated to the St. Francis River country in southeast Missouri. During the winter of 1811-12 this branch moved to the Arkansas Territory, where they were domiciled until a survey of the Cherokee Nation, Arkansas, was made by the United States Government in 1819 in accordance with the provisions of the Treaty of 1817.

Bowles' village was located between Shoal and Petit Jean Creeks, on the south side of Arkansas River, outside of the stipulated Cherokee Territory; on account of this fact and in compliance with the wishes of his followers to locate in Spanish territory, he, with sixty families, migrated in the winter of 1819-20 to territory that was claimed to have been promised them by the representatives of the Dominion of Spain, on Sabine River and extending from the Angelina to the Trinity Rivers in the Province of Texas.

Settlement was made north of Nacogdoches, then an expanse of waste and ruin, the result of warfare waged between the American and Spanish forces of Long and Perez. The climatic conditions auguring favorable to the pursuits of agriculture, stock-raising and hunting, their numbers were augmented occasionally by recruits from their brethren in Arkansas and other tribes of Indians in the United States.

For one whole year the Cherokees lived in peace and happiness under the roof of the hospitable Spaniard. Whether title to the lands accorded to and occupied by them was by prescription rights, the Indian mode of occupancy or in fee from the Monarch of Spain, is immaterial – they were there; their rights undisputed, under the impression they had a perfected right.

The Mexicans, their authority emanating from the imperial government at Mexico City, becoming dissatisfied with Spanish suzerainty over this portion of Latin America, adopted drastic measures toward throwing off the Spanish yoke.

By the plan of Iguala, adopted by the revolutionary government of Mexico, 24th February, 1821, the Mexicans published to the world that "all inhabitants of New Spain, without distinction, whether Europeans, Africans or Indians, are citizens of the monarchy, with a right to be employed in any post, according to their merit and virtues", and that "The person and property of every citizen will be respected and protected by the government". The Treaty of Cordova, of the 24th August, 1821, and the Declaration of Independence of the 28th September, 1821, reaffirmed the principles of the

3

THE TEXAS CHEROKEES
1820 – 1839.

Plan of Iguala. Also, the decree of the 24th February, 1822, by which "the sovereign congress of Mexico declares the equality of civil rights to all free inhabitants of the Empire, whatever may be their origin in the four quarters of the earth". Also, the decree of the 9th April, 1823, which reaffirmed the three guaranties of the Plan of Iguala, viz: - 1. Independence; 2. The Catholic religion; 3. Union of all Mexicans of whatever race. The decree of the 17th September, 1822, with a view to give effect to the 12th Article of the Plan of Iguala, declared that classification of the inhabitants with regard to their origin, shall be omitted. The foregoing solemn declarations of the political power of the government, had the effect, necessarily, of investing the Indians with the full privileges of citizenship, as effectually as had the Declaration of Independence of the United States of 1776 of vesting all those persons with these privileges, residing in the country at the time.

Under the constitution and laws of Mexico, as a race, no distinction was made between the Indians, as to rights of citizenship and the privileges belonging to it and those of European or Spanish blood. The Mexican Republic, from the time of its emancipation from Spain, always dealt most liberally with foreigners, in its anxiety to colonize its vacant lands. Where the grant declared that a citizen of the United States had been naturalized, it was taken for true. Thus, it will be seen during this transitory period in the political affairs of the country, the Cherokees bore the status of full-fledged citizens of the Republic of Mexico, with all the privileges and immunities attached to the other inhabitants thereof. The first evidence of any attempt at acquiring legal title to the lands occupied since their advent, is adduced by a letter from Richard Fields to James Dill, Alcalde of Nacogdoches, as follows:

"February 1st, 1822.

Dear Sir: I wish to fall at your feet and humbly ask you what must be done with us poor Indians? We have some grants that were given us when we lived under Spanish Government, and we wish you to send us news by the next mail whether they will be reversed or not. And if we were permitted, we will come as soon as possible to present ourselves before you in a manner agreeable to our talents. If we present ourselves in a rough manner, we pray you to right us. Our intentions are good toward the government.

Yours as a Chief of the Cherokee Nation,

Richard Fields."

4

THE TEXAS CHEROKEES
1820 – 1839.

[Early History of the Cherokees, page 177]

It appears that this communication went unanswered but was forwarded to the Governor of the province of Texas at Bexar or San Antonio.

An indisputable title or unquestioned right of occupancy was desired on their part. With this object in view, a delegation repaired to Bexar and on the 8th November, 1822, an agreement was entered into between the Cherokees and Jose Felex Trespalacios, Governor of the Province and acting for the Republic of Mexico.

"Articles of Agreement, made and entered into between Captain Richard (Fields) of the Cherokee Nation, and the Governor of the Province of Texas.

"Article 1.   That said Captain Richard (Fields) with five others of his tribe, accompanied by Mr. Antonio Mexia and Antonio Wolfe, who act as interpreters, may proceed to Mexico, to treat with his Imperial Majesty, relative to the settlement which said Chief wishes to make for those of his tribe who are already in the territory of Texas, and also for those who are in the United States.

"Art. 2nd.   That the other Indians in the city, and who do not accompany the before mentioned, will return to their village in the vicinity of Nacogdoches, and communicate to those who are at said village, the terms of this agreement.

"Art. 3rd.   That a party of warriors of said village must be constantly kept on the road leading from the province to the United States, to prevent stolen animals from being carried thither, and to apprehend and punish those evil disposed foreigners, who form assemblages, and abound on the banks of the River Sabine within the territory of Texas.

"Art. 4th.   That the Indians who return to their town will appoint as their chief, the Indian Captain called Kunetand, alias Tong Turqui, to whom a copy of this agreement will be given, for the satisfaction of those of his tribe, and in order that they may fulfill its stipulations.

"Art. 5th.   That meanwhile, and until the approval of the Supreme Government is obtained, they may cultivate their lands and sow their crops in free and possession.

"Art. 6th.   That the said Cherokee Indians will become immediately subject to the laws of the Empire, as well as others who tread her soil, and they will also take up arms in defense of the nation, if called upon to do so.

"Art. 7th.   That they shall be considered Hispano-Americans, and entitled to all the rights and privileges granted to such, and to the same protection, should it become necessary.

5

THE TEXAS CHEROKEES
1820 – 1839.

"Art. 8th.   That they can immediately commence trade with the other inhabitants of the province, and with the exception of arms and ammunitions of war, with the tribes of savages who may be friendly with us.

"Which agreement, comprising the eight preceeding articles, has been executed in the presence of twenty-two Cherokee Indians of the Baron de Bastrop, who has been pleased to act as interpreter, of two of the Ayuntamiento, and two officers of this Garrison.

Bexar, 8th – November, 1822.

> Jose Felix Trespalacios
> Jose Flores
> Nabor Villarreal
> Richard Fields X His Mark
> El Baron de Bastrop
> Manual Iturri Castillo
> Franco de Castanedo"

(Translations of Empresario Contracts, 85; Texas General Land Office)

In pursuance of this agreement Governor Trespalacios addressed the following communication to Don Gaspar Lopez, Commandant of the Eastern Internal Provinces, sending it by Lieutenant Don Ignacio Ronquillo:

"Captain Richard (Fields) of the Cherokee Nation, with twenty-two more Indians that accompanied him, visited me to ask permission for all belonging to his tribe, to settle upon the lands of this province. After I had been informed myself through foreigners, who are acquainted with this nation, that it is the most industrious and useful of the tribes in the United States, I entered with said Captain, into an agreement, the original of which I send you. This arrangement provided that Captain Richard and six others of his nation, with two interpreters, escorted by Lieutenant Don Ignacio Ronquillo and fifteen men of the Viscayan, shall proceed to your headquarters and, if it meet your approval, thence to the court of the Empire.

"The Cherokee Nation, according to their statement, numbers fifteen thousand souls; but there are within the borders of Texas only one hundred warriors and two hundred women and children. They work for their living, and dress in cotton-cloth, which they themselves manufacture. They raise cattle and horses and use firearms. Many of them understand the English language. In my opinion, they ought to be useful to the province, for they immediately became subject to its laws, and I believe will succeed in putting a stop to carrying stolen animals to the United States, and in arresting those evil-doers that infest the roads."

From the foregoing agreement and communication, it will be seen that the matter of procuring title was only partially and temporarily realized.

6

THE TEXAS CHEROKEES
1820 – 1839.

While occupation or prescription rights were accorded by the authorities, they were also recognized as Hispano-Americans and were clothed with judicial as well as police powers, pledging their unqualified support in time of war. They were recognized as agriculturists, manufacturers and stock-raisers and were to apprehend and try offenders against the laws of the Empire.

[Early History of the Cherokees, page 180]

Not being satisfied with conditions as to land titles, it was their determination to push their claims for a more satisfactory arrangement. Repairing to Saltillo, headquarters of the Commandant General, they were sent, early in December, on their way to Mexico City, where they arrived in the Spring of 1823. The conditions of the country were chaotic. The throne of Emperor Iturbide toppled and he was succeeded by Victoria, Bravo and Negrete on March 30th, 1823, who held the reigns of government, exercising a joint regency.

During the progress of affairs, Fields and his fellow-companions were detained, awaiting the decision of the government. The Minister of Relations gave notice that the agreement entered into between Fields and Trespalacios would be recognized, pending the passage of a general colonization law. The Minister of Relations, Lucas Alaman, in the new provisional government, wrote to Don Felipe de la Garza, the successor of Lopez, as Commandant General of the Eastern Internal Provinces as follows:

"The supreme Executive Power has been pleased to resolve that Richard Fields, Chief of the Cherokee Tribe of Indians, and his companions, now in this Capitol, may return to their country, and that they be supplied with whatever may be necessary for that purpose. Therefore, Their Supreme Highnesses have directed me to inform you that, although the agreement made on the 8th – November, 1822, between Richard Fields and Colonel Felix Trespalacios, Governor of Texas, remains provisionally in force, you are nevertheless required to be very careful and vigilant in regard to their settlements, endeavoring to bring them towards the interior, and at places least dangerous, not permitting for the present, the entrance of any new families of the Cherokee tribe, until the publication of the General Colonization Law, which will establish the rules and regulations to be observed, although the benefits to arise from it cannot be extended to them, in relation to all of which Their Highnesses intend to consult the Sovereign Congress. That while this is effecting, the families already settled should be well treated, and the other chiefs, also, treated with suitable consideration, provided that those already within our territory respect our laws, and are submissive to our authorities; and, finally, Their Highnesses order, that in future neither these Indians, nor any others, be permitted to come to the City of Mexico, but only send their petitions in ample form, for journeys similar to the present are of no benefit and only create unnecessary expense to the state. All of which I communicate to you for your information and fulfillment."

That the delegation regarded their land titles secure, is apparent. They returned home seemingly satisfied with their accomplishments. Victoria, Bravo and Negrete, through their Minister of Relations, had confirmed the then existing contract until such time that a general colonization law was enacted, implying that titles would be more securely vested under such a law.

About a year later, Fields proposed a union of all the Indian tribes in Eastern Texas, proposing to exact a pledge from them, of fidelity to the government. In promulgating this, he gave a summary of his accomplishments in Mexico City and of his plans for the future. On March 6th, 1824, he wrote to the Governor at San Antonio, as follows:

"It was my intention, on my return from Mexico, to present myself at San Antonio, in order that the authorities there might examine the papers which I received from the Superior Government of the Nation; but it was impossible to do so, because a party of Comanches had prepared an ambush on the road. However, I had the good fortune to escape them.

"The Superior Government has granted me in this province, a territory sufficient for me and that part of the tribe of Indians dependent on me to settle on, and also a commission to command all the Indians tribes and nations that are in the four eastern provinces.

"I pray your honor to notify all the Indians within your territory, and particularly the Lipans, that on the 4th of July next, I shall, in compliance with the order of the Supreme Government, hold a general council of all the Indian tribes, at my house in the rancheria of the Cherokees, twelve miles west of the Sabine River. At this Council, I shall propose a treaty of peace to all Indians who are willing to submit themselves to the orders of the government. In case there should be any who may not wish to ratify what I propose, I shall use force of arms to subdue them.

"I beg you to notify the commandant at San Antonio that he shall, for the satisfaction of his people, send some trusted person to aid in the treaty of peace and see how the affair is managed.

"Should it be convenient, have this letter translated and have the authorities send it to Rio Grande and Monclova, in which two places I left copies of the documents from the Superior Government."

The Grand Council took place in pursuance of call, with exception of the date which was changed to August 20th, 1824. All the tribes convened in council at Fields' residence, with the exception of the Comanches and Tonkawas, on whom he proposed to make war.

Closely following these events, the 24th – January, 1823, the Central Government under Augustine, the first constituted Emperor of Mexico, enacted the Imperial Colonization Law of 1823, which decreed, among other

THE TEXAS CHEROKEES
1820 – 1839.

things – "that the Mexican Government will protect the liberty, property and civil rights of all foreigners, etc." This was followed by the National Colonization Law of August 18, 1824, in which it was decreed – "To all who shall see and understand these presents – That the Mexican Nation offers to foreigners, who come to establish themselves within its territory, security for their persons and property, provided, they subject themselves to the laws of the country, etc., "and for this purpose, the legislature of all the states will, as soon as possible, form colonization laws, or regulations for their respective states, conforming themselves in all things to the constitutional act, general constitution, and the regulations established in this law, etc."

In pursuance of the foregoing, the State of Coahuila and Texas passed a colonization law March 25th, 1825, the first article of which reads:

"All foreigners who, in virtue of the general law of the 18th of August, 1824, which guarantees the security of their persons and property in this republic, shall wish to emigrate to any of the settlements of the State of Coahuila and Texas, are permitted to do so; and the said state invites and calls them." Second; "Those who shall thus emigrate, far from being molested, shall be admitted by the local authorities of said settlements, and permitted by the same to freely engage in any honest pursuit, provided they respect the general laws of the republic, and the laws of the state."

It is noticeable that the provisions of the three consecutive colonization laws, the word "foreigners" and the phrase "those who shall thus emigrate" would apply to those who arrived after their passage, the first, the Imperial, decreed the 4th of January, 1823. For the sake of clearness, it is deemed advisable to reiterate that the Cherokees were Mexican citizens and had been prior to the passage of these laws, as much so as any others who emigrated to Texas and were so made by statute or constitutional enactment.

Possibly, owing to the absence of the locomotive, telegraph and other modes of travel and conveniences of communication, many of the early settlers of Texas did not know of the passage of these laws, or whether the vested rights of the Cherokees were purposely ignored on the part of the authorities, is immaterial. The authorities of Coahuila and Texas, sitting at Saltilla, made divers and sundries grants of lands. These embraced portions of Cherokee territory, and among the donors were David G. Burnet, Vincente Filisola, Robert Leftwich, Frost Thorn and the Edwards Brothers. This act so incensed the Cherokees, that a council was soon after convened. Peter Ellis Bean reported to Stephen F. Austin that Fields addressed the council substantially as follows:

"In my old days, I traveled two thousand miles to the City of Mexico to beg some lands to settle a poor orphan tribe of Red People, who looked to me for protection. I was promised lands for them after staying one year in Mexico and spending all I had. I then came to my people and waited two years, and then send Mr. Hunter, after selling my stock to provide him money

9

for his expenses. When he got there, he stated his mission to the government. They said they knew nothing of this Richard Fields and treated him with contempt.

"I am a Red Man and a man of honor and can't be imposed on this way. We will lift up our tomahawks and fight for land with all those friendly tribes that wish land also. If I am beaten, I will resign to fate, and if not, I will hold lands by the force of my red warriors."

John Dunn Hunter, a white man, had come among the Cherokees sometime during the year 1825. Through his intervention, hope was held out that the agitated question of land title would be amicably settled. With this end in view, he was dispatched to Mexico City to plead their cause. He arrived at the seat of government March 19th, 1826 and returned in September, after fruitless attempts at a settlement of title.

Seeing their lands taken possession of by new-comers, their homes and fire-sides so long established, what they considered wrongfully wrested from them, they began to prepare to maintain their holdings peacefully, if possible, but by force, if they must. Touching these events, Stephen F. Austin wrote the Commander of Texas September 11, 1826 in part, as follows:

"There is reason to fear that the delay of the measures concerning the peaceable tribes has disgusted them; and should this be the case, it would be a misfortune, for 100 of the Cherokees are worth more as warriors than 500 Comanches."

Hunter, "pictured in story and glowing language the gloomy alternative, now plainly presented to the Indians, of abandoning their present abodes and returning within the limits of the United States – or preparing to defend themselves against the whole power' of the Mexican Government by force of arms------------"

John G. Purnell wrote to Fields from Saltillo on October 4th, 1825, as follows:

"When I last saw you in my house at Monterey, I little thought in so short a time you would have commenced a war against your American brothers and the Mexican Nation; more particularly a man like yourself who is acquainted with the advantages of civilization.------ If your claims for lands were not granted at a time when the government was not firmly established, that should not be a cause of war. Ask and it will be given to you; this nation has always felt friendly inclined toward yours, and I am sure if you cease hostilities they will enter into a treaty with you by which you will obtain more permanent advantages than you can by being at war-----."

On November 10th, 1825, F. Durcy, also of Saltillo , wrote to Francis Grapp, a well-known Indian trader at Natchitoches:

"Knowing the weight of your influence with all the savage nations and also the ascendancy that you have over the character of Mr. Fields, your son-in-law, I think that no one could stop, better than yourself, the great disturbance which is about to be raised by the Indians, whom you understand better than I. I say that you can distinguish yourself for the welfare of humanity in general, in making the savages understand the evils which await them in following the plans of Mr. Fields, and likewise causing Mr. Fields to be spoken to by his brother, who can prevail upon him (le determiner) to abandon a plan which will have no other end than that of destroying himself and all those who shall have the misfortune to follow him."

Hunter's mission to Mexico City failed of its purpose. The Edwards brothers, who had been granted territory on which to settle eight hundred families, discovered that their claim of title conflicted with others originating under the Spanish regime. These lands also over-lapped the Cherokee cessions. They had consumed large sums of money, time, and an enormous amount of work in the United States arranging for the introduction of the eight hundred families called for by the terms of the empresario contract with the Mexican government. Finding themselves in dispute over their lands, almost the same as their neighbors, the Cherokees, affairs were rapidly reaching a critical stage in that portion of Texas.

The Edwards, highly incensed at the prospects of losing their all at one fell swoop, determined to throw off Mexican sovereignty and thus declare Texas a free and independent nation, under the name of the Republic of Fredonia.

Fields and Hunter concluded to confer with this embryo government on future plans. On their arrival at Nacogdoches, they found all excitement and chaos. A compact was entered into by Fields and Hunter, on the part of the Red people, and Harmon B. Mayo and Benjamin W. Edwards, as agents of the committee of Independence, culminating into a solemn Union, League and Confederation in peace and war to establish and defend their independence against Mexico.

The compact entered into, follows:

"Whereas, the Government of the Mexican United States have, by repeated insults, treachery and oppression, reduced the White and Red emigrants from the United States of North America, now living in the Province of Texas, within the territory of said government, which they have been deluded by promises solemnly made, and most basely broken, to the dreadful alternative of either submitting their free-born necks to the yoke of the imbecile, unfaithful, and despotic government, miscalled a Republic, or of taking up arms in defense of their inalienable rights and asserting their independence; they – viz: The White emigrants now assembled in the town of Nacogdoches, around the independent standard, on the one part, and the Red emigrants who have espoused the same Holy Cause, on the other, in order to prosecute more speedily and effectually the War of Independence, they have mutually undertaken, to a successful issue, and to bind themselves by the ligaments of reciprocal interests and obligations, have resolved to form a treaty of Union, League and Confederation.

"For this illustrious object, Benjamin W. Edwards and Harmon B. Mayo, Agents of the Committee of Independence, and Richard Fields and John D. Hunter, the agents of the Red people, being respectfully furnished with due powers, have agreed to the following articles:

"1.   The above named contracting parties, bind themselves to a solemn Union, League, and Confederation, in peace and war, to establish and defend their mutual independence of the Mexican United States.

"2.   The contracting parties guaranty, mutually to the extent of their power, the integrity of their respective territories, as now agreed upon and described, viz: The territory apportioned to the Red people, shall begin at the Sandy Spring, where Bradley's road takes off from the road leading from Nacogdoches to the Plantation of Joseph Dust; from thence west by the compass, without regard to variation, to the Rio Grande; thence to the head of the Rio Grande; thence with the mountains to the head of the Big Red River; thence north to the boundary of the United States of America; thence with the same line to the mouth of Sulphur Fork; thence in a right line to the beginning.

"The territory apportioned to the White people, shall comprehend all the residue of the Province of Texas, and of such other portions of the Mexican United States, as the contracting parties, by their mutual efforts and resources, may render independent, provided the same shall not extend further west than the Rio Grande.

"3.   The contracting parties mutually guaranty the rights of Empresarios to their premium lands only, and the rights of all other individuals, acquired under the Mexican Government and relating or appertaining to the above described territory, provided the said Empresarios and individuals do not forfeit the same by an opposition to the independence of the said territories, or by withdrawing their aid and support to its accomplishment.

"4.   It is distinctly understood by the contracting parties, that the territory apportioned to the Red people is intended as well for the benefit of those tribes now settled in the territory apportioned to the White people, as for those living in the former territory, and that it is incumbent upon the contracting parties for the Red people to offer the said tribes a participation in the same.

"5.   It is also mutually agreed by the contracting parties, that every individual, Red or White, who has made improvements within either of the Respective Allied Territories and lives upon the same, shall have a fee simple of a section of land, including his improvement, as well as the protection of the government in which he may reside.

"6.   The contracting parties mutually agree, that all roads, navigable streams, and all other channels of conveyance within each Territory, shall be open and free to the use of the inhabitants of the other.

"7.   The contracting parties mutually stipulate that they will direct all their resources to the prosecution of the heaven-inspired caused which has given birth to this solemn Union, League and Confederation, firmly relying upon their united efforts, and the strong arm of Heaven for success.

"In faith whereof, the Agents of the respective contracting parties hereunto affix their names.

"Done in the town of Nacogdoches, this the twenty-first day of December, in the year of our Lord, one thousand eight hundred and twenty-six."

Richard Fields	B.W. Edwards
John D. Hunter	H.B. Mayo

"We, the Committee of Independence, and the Committee of the Red people, do ratify the above Treaty, and do pledge ourselves to maintain it in good faith.

"Done on the day and date above mentioned.

Richard Fields	Martin Parmer, President
John D. Hunter	Hayden Edwards
Ne-Ko-Lake	W.B. Legon
John Bags	John Sprowl
Cuk-To-Keh	B.J. Thompson
	Jos. A. Huber
	B.W. Edwards
	H.B. Mayo

While these things were transpiring in and around Nacogdoches, the Mexicans, with their chief allies, Stephen F. Austin and Peter Ellis Bean, were stirring up dissatisfaction among the Fredonians, both Red and White people. To forestall any further preparations on the part of the infant revolutionary government, Bean, on 16th – December, arrived with thirty-five Mexican soldiers from San Antonio. On learning of the feelings that pervaded the Fredonians, he retired to a point west of Nacogdoches to await reinforcements, realizing his forces were inadequate to successfully cope with the revolutionary forces. About the 20th of the same month, two hundred strong under Colonel Mateo Ahumada, with banners flying, the glittering of steel and the clanking of arms, marched out of San Antonio, bent on the conquest of Nacogdoches. This contingent was accompanied by Jose Antonio Saucedo, the Political Chief, in full charge of operations.

On January 22nd – 1826, Austin addressed the Mexican people in terms, as follows:
"To the Inhabitants of the Colony:

"The persons who were sent on from this colony by the Political Chief and Military Commandant (Austin) to offer peace to the madmen of Nacogdoches, have returned – returned without having affected anything. The olive branch of peace which was held out to them has been insultingly returned, and that party have announced massacre and desolation to this colony. They are trying to excite al the Northern Indians to murder and plunder, and it appears as though they have no other object than to ruin and plunder this country. They openly threaten us with massacre and the plunder of our property.

"To arms then, my friends and fellow-citizens, and hasten to the standard of our country.
"The first hundred men will march on the 26th.
Necessary orders for mustering and other purposes will be issued to commanding officers.

Union and Mexico.

S.F. Austin.

San Felipe de Austin,
January 27th – 1827."

The authorities and leading citizens of Austin's Colony lost no time in fomenting dissension in the ranks of the Fredonians. From the capitol of his colony, Austin hurled all the epithets at his command against his liberty-loving American brothers. Writers of Texan history condemn him for the course taken in this instance. A careful perusal of the compact entered into by the Fredonians will not disclose an iota justifying his denunciations in such terms, in his proclamation to the colonists. The compact was to them, what the immortal document of 1776 was to the Americans during the gloomy days of the American Revolution. It was their divorcement from a weak, unstable and vacillating rule. It was the forerunner of the glory of San Jacinto, the climax that thrills the heart of every loyal Texan and freeman throughout Christiandom[sic]. Doomed to failure it was, and the perpetrators suffered the consequences.

14

THE TEXAS CHEROKEES
1820 – 1839.

Their propaganda was successful. Promises of land and other preferments by Bean and Austin detached large numbers of the Fredonians, leaving the loyal in a hopeless state. Bowles and Mush, of the Cherokees, were among the detached. Due to their machinations, Fields and Hunter were foully murdered by men of their own people. The Edwards contingent was dispersed and fled to Louisiana, and other portions of the United States. For his services in having Fields and Hunter put out of the way, Bowles was invested with a commission as nominal Colonel in the Mexican army, as was also Peter Ellis Bean. The Fredonian affair was terminated.

Affairs in this portion of Texas were restored to normalcy, with the exception of the mooted question of land titles. To further complicate matters, the legislature made a division of the territory in question between David G. Burnet and Joseph Vehlein.

The Act of April 6th, 1830, prohibiting the further emigration of Americans into Texas, was passed. General Teran, Commandant General of the Eastern Interior States, determined to perfect title in the Cherokees, to lands so long occupied by them, and on August 15th, 1831, wrote to Letona, Governor of Coahuila and Texas:

"In compliance with the promises made by the Supreme Government, to the Cherokee Indians, and with a view to the preservation of peace, with the rude tribes, I caused them to determine upon some fixed spot for their settlement, and having selected it on the head waters of the Trinity, and the banks of the Sabine, I pray your Excellency may be pleased to order that possession be given to them, with the corresponding titles, with the understanding that it will be expedient, that the commissioners be appointed for this purpose, should act in conjunction with Colonel Jose de las Piedras, commanding the military force on the frontier of Nacogdoches."

Teran's suggestions that title be consummated was universally concurred in by the authorities. March 22, 1832, Governor Letona ordered the political chief to furnish Commissioner Piedras with the necessary documents in due form for that purpose. On the eve of preparations to carry out such orders, he was expelled from Nacogdoches by an uprising of Americans. Soon afterwards, Teran committed suicide and was succeeded in office by Vincente Filisola who held an impresario contract in his own name. This appointment was detrimental to the interests of the Cherokees in the extreme, because his contract embraced a portion of their lands. Governor Letona died of yellow fever and was succeeded by Peramendi.

The attempts on the part of Mexico to grant title, ended with these transactions.

On July 20th, 1833, a delegation headed by Colonel Bowles repaired to San Antonio and petitioned the Political Chief for title to their lands. They were directed to Monclova, the Capitol of the Province of Coahuila and

THE TEXAS CHEROKEES
1820 – 1839.

Texas, where they were given assurance that their claims would receive due consideration. But, inasmuch as David G. Burnet and Vincente Filisola had immatured colonization contracts which were to expire December 21st-1835, all land title he maintained must, of necessity, be held in abeyance for the time being. However, on March 10th-1835, the Political Chief wrote the Supreme Government, admonishing the authorities that the Cherokees be not disturbed in their possessions until the central government at Mexico City could finally pass on the question.

On May 12, 1835, the Legislature of the State of Coahuila and Texas passed the following resolution:

"Art. 1. In order to secure the peace and tranquility of the state, the government is authorized to select, out of the vacant lands of Texas, that land which may appear most appropriate for the location of the peaceable and civilized Indians which may have been introduced into Texas.

"Art. 2. It shall establish with them a line of defense along the frontier to secure the state against the incursions of barbarous tribes."

This was the last utterance of the Mexican Government in reference to the Cherokee claims.

At the beginning of the disaffection of the Americans, the Committee of Public Safety, the Permanent Council and the Consultation, successively, had deemed it just and prudent to arrive at some understanding with the Cherokees and other Indians concerning their land claims.

The state of affairs at this period existing between the Central Government at Mexico City and the State of Coahuila and Texas was exceedingly critical. On the 19th of September, 1835, on behalf of the Committee of Safety, Stephen F. Austin addressed the people of Texas in part: "That every district should send members to the General Consultation, with full powers to do whatever may be necessary for the good of the country."

The General Consultation convened on the 16th – October, 1835, but adjourned for want of a quorum. It reassembled at San Felipe de Austin on November 1st, but was unable to dispatch business until the 3rd, when a quorum appeared. Dr. Branch T. Archer of Brazoria, formerly Speaker of the House of Delegates kellin the Virginia Legislature, was unanimously elected President. This was the third deliberative body authorized on the American plan, superseding the conventions of October 1, 1832, and April 1, 1833. In an elaborate speech to the convention, President Archer reviewed the condition of affairs of the country and recommended plans upon which Texas was to erect autonomy and at the same time contest upon the field of battle for a long-cherished independence. Among other things impressed upon the members of the Consultation, were the need of establishing a provisional Government, with a Governor, Lieutenant Governor and Council to be clothed with Legislative and executive powers; and that "there are several

THE TEXAS CHEROKEES
1820 – 1839.

warlike and peaceful tribes of Indians that claim certain portions of our land. Locations have been made within the limits they claim, which has created great dissatisfaction amongst them. Some of the chiefs of those tribes are expected here in a few days, and I deem it expedient to make some equitable arrangement of the matter that will prove satisfactory to them."

On the 7th of November, 1835, the Unanimous Declaration of the Consultation was adopted. It declared that "General Lopez de Santa Anna and other military chieftains have, by force of arms, overthrown the federal institutions of Mexico and dissolved the social compact which existed between Texas and other members of the Mexican Confederacy; Now, the good people of Texas, availing themselves of their natural rights, Solemnly Declare – 1st. That they have taken up arms in defense of their Rights and Liberties, -----."

In pursuance of this Declaration of Independence, a Plan or Constitution for a Provisional Government was drawn by a committee headed by Henry Smith, reported to that body on November 9th, but was not adopted as the organic act until the 11th, at which time it was enrolled and signed. A provisional Government was thus created; among the prerogatives or duties imposed upon the Governor and Council were to hypothecate the public lands and pledge the public faith for a loan not to exceed one million dollars; to impose and regulate imports and tonnage duties and provide for the collection of the same; treat with the several tribes of Indians in reference to their land titles, and, if possible, to secure their friendship; establish post offices and post-roads; regulate postal rates and appoint a post-master general; grant pardons and hear admiralty cases.

Adoption of this plan and the election of officers took place on November 12th, and signed by the fifty-four delegates present on the following day. Henry Smith, opposed by S.F. Austin, was duly elected Provisional Governor, while James W. Robinson of Nacogdoches, was elected Lieutenant Governor.

From the time of the conception of a separation of Texas from Mexico, it was deemed advisable to conciliate the Indian Tribes within her borders, and this could best be brought about by entering into a treaty of friendship and neutrality and at the same time guarantee to them title to the lands occupied. The Cherokees were peacefully domiciled in east central Texas and were regarded, and justly so, as agriculturists, manufacturers, stock-raisers and the followers of other pursuits that well placed them out of the savage or hunter class and compelled the fitting appellation of Civilized Indians. They possessed, as a nation, several hundred soldiers or warriors who were expert riflemen.

On November 13th, 1835, the day of the adoption of the Plans and Powers or the Constitution of the Provisional Government, the following

Solemn Declaration was unanimously adopted and signed by the entire body of fifty-four members:

"Be It Solemnly Decreed, That we, the chosen delegates of the Consultation of the people of all Texas, in general convention assembled, solemnly declare that the Cherokee Indians, and their associate bands, twelve tribes in number, agreeable to their last general council in Texas, have derived their just claims to lands, included within the bounds hereinafter mentioned from the government of Mexico, from whom we have also derived our rights to the soil by grant and occupancy.

(Title of lands guaranteed by Provisional Government of Texas, to Cherokees, in 1826.)

"We solemnly declare that the boundaries of the claims of the said Indians to land is as follows, to-wit: Lying north of the San Antonio road and the Neches, and west of the Angelina and Sabine Rivers. We solemnly declare that the Governor and General Council, immediately on its organization, shall appoint Commissioners to treat with the said Indians, to establish the definite boundaries of their territory, and secure their confidence and friendship.

"We solemnly declare that we will guarantee to them the peaceful enjoyment of their rights to their lands, as we do our own; we solemnly declare, that all grants, surveys and locations of lands, hereinbefore mentioned, made after the settlements of said Indians, are, and of right ought to be, utterly null and void, and that the Commissioners issuing the same, be and are hereby ordered, immediately to recall and cancel the same, as having been made upon lands already appropriated by the Mexican Government.

"We solemnly declare that it is our sincere desire that the Cherokee Indians, and their associate bands, should remain our friends in peace and war, and if they do so, we pledge the public faith for the support of the foregoing declarations.

"We solemnly declare that they are entitled to our commiseration and protection, as the just owners of the soil, as an unfortunate race of people, that we wish to hold as friends, and treat with justice. Deeply and solemnly impressed with these sentiments as a mark of sincerity, your committee would respectfully recommend the adoption of the following resolution:

"Resolved, that the members of this convention, now present, sign this declaration, and pledge the public faith, on the part of the people of Texas.

"Done in Convention at San Felipe de Austin, this 13th – day of November, A.D. 1835.

THE TEXAS CHEROKEES
1820 – 1839.

(Signed) B.T. Archer, President,
John A. Wharton, Meriwether W. Smith, Sam Houston, William Menifee, Chas. Wilson, Wm. N. Sigler, James Hodges, Wm. W. Arrington, John Bevil, Wm. S. Fisher, Alex. Thompson, J.G.V. Pierson, D.C. Barrett, R. Jones, Jesse Burnham, Lorenzo de Zavala, A. Horton, Edwin Waller, Daniel Parker, Wm. P. Harris, John S.D. Byrom, Wm. Whitaker, A.G. Perry, Albert G. Kellogg, C.C. Dyer, Geo. M. Patrick, J.D. Clements, Claiborne West, Jas. W. Parker, J.S. Lester, Geo. W. Davis, Joseph L. Wood, A.E.C. Johnson, Asa Hoxey, Martin Parmer, Asa Mitchell, L.H. Everett, R.M. Williamson, Phillip Coe, R.R. Royal, John W. Moore, Benj. Fuga, Sam T. Allen, Wyatt Hanks, James W. Robinson, Henry Millard, Jesse Grimes, A.B. Hardin, Wyly Martin, Henry Smith, David A. Macomb, A. Houston, E. Collard.

P.B. Dexter,
Secretary."

Pledging the public faith on the part of the people of Texas, among other things the "Solemn Declaration", after defining the boundaries of the claims of the Cherokees enunciated "that we will guarantee to them the peaceful enjoyment of their rights to their lands, as we do our own, we solemnly declare that all grants, surveys and locations of lands, within the bounds hereinbefore mentioned, made after the settlement of said Indians, are, and of right ought to be, utterly null and void, and that the commissioners issuing the same, be and are hereby ordered, immediately to recall and cancel the same, as having been made upon lands already appropriated by the Mexican Government."

After the passage of the Colonization Laws, giving to the respective states the right to make disposition of the vacant lands within their boundaries, it will be remembered that David G. Burnet and others were awarded contracts affecting lands within the boundaries described and partially in the Cherokee Nation.

When the Consultation was published to the world, it was then just a little over a month until the date of the expiration of the contracts of Burnet and Filasola, which fell on December 21, 1835. "And all grants, surveys and locations of lands within the bounds hereinbefore mentioned, made after the settlement of said Indians, are, and of right ought to be, null and void."

As has been said, the Cherokees settled on these lands in the winter of 1819-20, while the contracts of Burnet bear date December 22,1826. All the acts of the Consultation were the basic or organic laws of the land and if any act is to be accepted as such, these contracts must certainly have been annulled, since their provisions bore directly upon lands already appropriated by the Mexican Government and so recognized by the Consultation and the

19

THE TEXAS CHEROKEES
1820 – 1839.

Provisional Government of Texas. "Language could not be made more plain or obligatory than was this guarantee to these tribes."

Among the several acts of this body, a Major General who was to be Commander-in-chief of all the Military forces, was elected by that body. Sam Houston was the unanimous choice. His commission follows:

"To Sam Houston, Esquire:

"In the name of the people of Texas, free and sovereign.

"We, reposing special trust and confidence in your patriotism, valor, conduct and fidelity, do by these presents constitute and appoint you to be Major General and Commander-in-chief of the armies of Texas and of all the forces now raised or to be raised by it, and of all others who shall voluntarily offer their services and join the army, for the defense of the constitution and liberty, and for repelling every hostile invasion thereof; and you are hereby vested with full power and authority to act as you shall think best for the good and welfare of the service.

"And we do hereby strictly charge and require all officers and soldiers under your command to be obedient to your orders, and diligent in the exercise of their several duties.

"And we do also enjoin you to be careful in executing the great trust reposed in you, by causing strict discipline and order to be observed in the army and that the soldiers be duly exercised, and provided with all convenient necessaries.

"And you are to regulate your conduct in every respect by the rules and discipline of war adopted by the United States of North America, or such as may be hereafter adopted by this government; and particularly to observe such orders and directions, from time to time, as you shall receive from this or a future government of Texas.

"This commission to continue in force until revoked by this or a future government.

"Done at San Felipe de Austin, on the fourteenth day of November, eighteen Hundred and thirty-five.

Henry Smith,
Governor.

P.B. Dexter, Secretary of
Provisional Government."

On November 14th, the Consultation ceased its labors. Governor Smith immediately convened the Council for the government of the country. Upon the organization of the Council, Governor Smith addressed that body the following letter relative to carrying into effect that portion of the Declaration touching the Cherokee claims:

"San Felipe, December 18, 1835.

Gentlemen of the Council:
"----------- I further have to suggest to you the propriety of appointing the commissioners on the part of this government to carry into affect the Indian treaty as contemplated by the Convention. I can see no difficulty which can reasonably occur in the appointment of the proper agents on our part, having so many examples and precedents before us. The United States have universally sent their most distinguished military officers to perform such duties, because the Indians generally look up to and respect their authority as coercive and paramount. I would therefore suggest the propriety of appointing General Houston, of the army, and Col. John Forbes of Nacogdoches, who has been already commissioned as one of my aides. The Commissioners would go specially instructed, so that no wrong could be committed either to the government, the Indians, or our individual citizens. All legitimate rights would be respected, and no others. I am well aware that we have no right to transcend the superior order, and Declaration made by the convention, and, if I recollect that article right, the outline of external boundaries was demarked within which the Indian tribes alluded to should be located; but at the same time paying due regard to the legitimate rights of the citizens within the same limits.

"If these Indians have introduced themselves in good faith under the Colonization Laws of the Government, they should be entitled to the benefits of those laws and comply with their conditions. I deem it a duty which we owe them to pay all due respect to their rights and claim their co-operation in the support of them and at the same time not to infringe upon the rights of our countrymen, so far as they have been justly founded.

"These agents going under proper instructions, would be enabled to do right, but not permitted to do wrong, as their negotiations would be subject to investigation and ratification by the government before they become a law.

I am, gentlemen,

Your Obedient Servant,

Henry Smith,

Governor."

Resolution appointing Commissioners to treat with the Cherokee Indians, etc.

"Be It Resolved by the General Council of the Provisional Government of Texas, That Sam Houston, John Forbes and John Cameron, be and they are hereby appointed Commissioners to treat with the Cherokee Indians, and their twelve Associate Bands, under such instructions as may be given them by the Governor and Council, and should it so happen that all the Commissioners cannot attend, any two of them shall have power to conclude a treaty and report the same to the General Council of the Provisional Government, for its approval and ratification.

"Be It Further Resolved, etc. That said Commissioners be required to hold said treaty so soon as practicable.

"Passed, Dec. 22d – 1835.

James W. Robinson,
Lieut-Gov. and ex-offico
Pres't. of G.C.

E.M. Pease,
Sec'y to General Council,
Approved, December 28, 1835.

Henry Smith, Governor.

C.B. Stewart,

Sec'y. to Executive."

Resolution for instructing Commissioners appointed   to treat with the Cherokee Indians and their Associate Bands:

"Be It Resolved by the General Council of the provisional Government of Texas, That Sam Houston, John Forbes and John Cameron, appointed Commissioners to treat with the aforesaid Indians, be and they are hereby instructed, to proceed as soon as practicable, to Nacogdoches, and hold a treaty with the Indians aforesaid, and that they shall in no wise transcend the Declarations made by the Consultation of November last, in any of their articles of treaty.

"Sec. 2. Be It Further Resolved, etc. That they are required in all things to pursue a course of justice and equity toward the Indians, and to protect all honest claims of the whites, agreeably to such laws, compacts or treaties, as the said Indians may have heretofore made with the Republic of Mexico, and that the (said) Commissioners be instructed to provide in said treaty with the Indians, that they shall never alienate their lands, either separately or collectively, except to the Government will at any time hereafter, purchase all their claims at a fair and reasonable valuation.

"Sec. 3. Be It Further Resolved, etc. That the Governor be required to give to the Commissioners, such definite and particular instructions as he may think necessary to carry into effect the object of the foregoing

THE TEXAS CHEROKEES
1820 – 1839.

resolutions, together with such additional instructions as will secure the effective co-operations of the Indians at a time when it may be necessary to call all the effective forces of Texas into the field, and agreeing for their services in a body for a specified time.

"Sec. 4. Be it Further Resolved, etc. That the Commissioners be authorized and empowered to exchange other lands within the limits of Texas, not otherwise appropriated in place of the lands claimed by said Cherokee Indians and their Associated Bands.

"Passed at San Felipe de Austin, Dec. 26, 1835.

James W. Robinson,
Lieut-Gov. and ex-officio Pres't of
(G.C.

E.M. Pease,
Secy. of General Council
C.B. Stewart, Sec'y of Executive

Henry Smith
Governor

Treaty Between the Commissioners on Behalf of the Provisional Government of Texas and the Cherokee Indians and Twelve Associate Tribes:

"This treaty this day made and established between Sam Houston and John Forbes, Commissioners on the one part, and the Cherokees and their associates bands now residing in Texas, of the other part, to wit: Shawnees, Delawares, Kickapoos, Quapaws, Choctaws, Boluxies, Jawanies, Alabamas, Cochaties, Caddoes of the Noches, Tahovcattakes, and Unatuqous---- , by the head chiefs and head men and warriors of the Cherokees, as elder brothers and representatives of all other bands, agreeable to their last council. This treaty is made in conformity to the declaration made by the last general consultation at San Felipe and dated the 13th – of November, 1835.

"Article 1. The parties declare that there shall be a firm and lasting peace forever, and that friendly intercourse shall be preserved by the people belonging to both parties.

"Article 2. It is agreed and declared that the before-mentioned tribes or bands shall form one community and that they shall have and possess the lands within the following bounds, to-wit: Lying west of the San Antonio road and beginning on the west at the point where the road crosses the river Angelina and running up said river until it reaches the first large creek below the great Shawnee Village emptying into said river from the northwest; thence running with said creek to its main source, and from thence a due northwest course to the Sabine river, and with said river west, then starting where the San Antonio road crosses the Angelina River, and with the said road to a point where it crosses the Neches River, and thence running up to the east side of said river in a northwest direction.

THE TEXAS CHEROKEES
1820 – 1839.

[There was no article 3 in this transcript.]

"Article 4. It is agreed by all parties that the several bands or their tribes named in this treaty shall all remove within the limits or bounds as above described.

"Article 5. It is agreed and declared by the parties aforesaid that the land lying and being within the aforesaid limits, shall never be sold or alienated to any person or persons, power or government whatsoever other than the government of Texas, bind themselves to prevent in the future all persons from intruding on said bounds. And it is agreed on the part of the Cherokees, for themselves and their younger brothers, that no other tribes or bands of Indians whatsoever shall settle within the limits aforesaid, but those already named in this treaty and now residing in Texas.

"Article 6. It is declared that no individual person, member of the tribes before named, shall have power to sell or lease land to any person or persons not a member or members of this community of Indians, nor shall any citizen of Texas be allowed to lease or buy land from any Indian or Indians.

"Article 7. That the Indians shall be governed by their own regulations and laws, within their own territory, not contrary to the laws of the Government of Texas. All property stolen from the citizens of Texas, or from the Indians shall be restored to the party from whom it was taken and the offender or offenders shall be punished by the party to whom he or they may belong.

"Article 8. The Government of Texas shall have power to regulate trade and intercourse, but no tax shall be laid on the trade of the Indians.

[There was no Article 9 in transcript.]

"Article 10. The parties to this treaty agree, that as soon as Jack Steele and Samuel Benge shall abandon their improvements without the limits of the before recited tract of country and remove within the same – that they shall be valued and paid for by the Government of Texas – the said Jack Steele and Samuel Benge having until the month of November, next succeeding from the date of this treaty, allowed them to remove within the limits before described. And that all the lands and improvements now occupied by any of the before named bands or tribes not lying within the limits before described, shall belong to the Government of Texas and subject to its disposal.

"Article 11. The parties to this treaty agree, and stipulate that all the bands or tribes, as before recited (except Steele and Benge) shall remove within the before described limits within eight months from the date of this treaty.

THE TEXAS CHEROKEES
1820 – 1839.

"Article 12. The parties to this treaty agree that nothing herein contained shall effect the relations of the neighborhood thereof, until a General Council of the several bands shall take place and the pleasure of the convention of Texas be known.

"Article 13. It is also declared, That all the titles issued to lands not agreeably to the Declaration of the General Consultation of the people of all Texas, dated the thirteenth day of November, eighteen hundred and thirty five, within the before recited limits – are declared void – as well as all orders and surveys made in relation to the same.

"Done at Colonel Bowl's Village on the twenty-third day of February, eighteen hundred and thirty-six, and the first year of the Provisional Government of Texas.

Signed:

Witness -   Sam Houston

                                               John Forbes
his   his
Fox X Fields   Colonel X Bowl
mark   mark
                                               his
Henry Millard   Big X Mush
                                               mark
                                               his
Joseph Durst   Samuel X Benge
                                               mark
A. Horton   his
                                               Oozovta X
                                               mark
George W. Case   his
                                               Corn X Tassell
Mathias A. Bingham   mark

George V. Hockley   his
                                               The X Egg
Sec'y of Commission   mark

                                               John Bowl

                                               his
                                               Tunnetoe X
                                               mark

THE TEXAS CHEROKEES
1820 – 1839.

Commissioners Sam Houston and John Forbes, on the part of the Provisional Government of Texas, reported as follows to the Governor:

Washington, February 29, 1836

To His Excellency,

Henry Smith, Governor of Texas

Sir:-

      In accordance with a commission issued by your Excellency dated the 25th day of December, 1835, the authorized commissioners, in the absence of John Cameron, Esquire, one of the commissioners named in the above mentioned instrument, most respectfully report: That after sufficient notice being given to the different tribes named in the commission, a treaty was held at the house of John _____ , one of the tribe of Cherokee Indians ---------- . The Commissioners would also suggest to your Excellency that titles should be granted to such actual settlers as are now within the designated boundaries, and that they should receive a fair remuneration for their improvements and the expenses attendant upon the exchange inlands or other equivalent.

      It will also be remembered by your Excellency that the surrender by the Government of the lands to which the Indians may have had any claims is nearly equivalent to that portion now allotted to them and we must respectfully suggest that they should be especially appropriated for the use of the government. They also call your attention to the following remarks, viz: "The state of excitement in which the Indians were first found by your commissioners, rendered it impossible to commence negotiations with them on the day set apart for it. On the day succeeding, the treaty was opened. Some difficulty then occurred relative to the exchange of lands, which the Commissioners proposed making for those now occupied by them, which was promptly rejected. The boundaries were those established as designated in the treaty alone and that such measures should be adopted by your Excellency for their security as may be deemed necessary---------. The Commissioners used every exertion to retain that portion of territory for the use of the government, but an adherence to this would have but one effect, viz: that of defeating the treaty altogether."

      "Under these circumstances the arrangement was made as now reported in the accompanying treaty. They would also suggest the importance of the salt works to the government and the necessity that they should be kept for the use of the government.

"The Commissioners also endeavored to enlist the chiefs of the different tribes in the cause of the people of Texas and suggested an enrollment of a force from them to act against our common enemy, in reply to which they informed us that the subject had not before been suggested to them, but a general council should be held in the course of the present month, when their determination will be made known.

"The expenses attendant upon the treaty are comparatively light, a statement of which will be furnished to your Excellency.

"All of which is most respectfully submitted.

Sam Houston,

John Forbes."

After about sixteen years the ambitions of the Cherokees to acquire undisputed title to their lands were at last realized. Their boundaries were definitely established; they were in a national existence, holding their lands in community or in common, living under laws of their own making, executed by their own officers without outside interference, living under the protection of the Government of Texas with one or more agents among them.

Without doubt, the main issue between them and the Spanish and Mexican authorities was that the Cherokees desired their lands in common, which was their method in the United States, while this policy was unknown to the two regimes mentioned and contrary to the Caucasian method of conveying title. However, their settled claims were held in abeyance until finally settled under the terms of the "Solemn Declaration" of November 13, 1835 and the foregoing treaty.

Immediately following the submission of the treaty and report, General Sam Houston repaired to and took command of the army on March 11, 1836.

On March 1 – the convention assembled and adopted the Declaration of Independence of Texas. On the following day, same was signed by the fifty-two members present; later six others appeared and signed, making the total, fifty-eight. The arrival of Provisional Governor Smith, the Lieutenant Governor and the remnant of the Council and the submission of the following report by the Provisional Governor, marked the

27

closing days of the Provisional Government and the institution of a new order:

"To the President and Members of the Convention of the People of Texas:
"Gentlemen: Called to the gubernational[sic] chair by your suffrages at the last Convention, I deem it a duty to lay before your honorable body a view, or outline of what has transpired since your last meeting, respecting the progress and administration of the government placed under my charge, as created and contemplated by the organic law.

"The Council, which was created to co-operate with me as the devisors of ways and means, having complied with all the duties assigned to them, by the third article of the Organic Law, was adjourned on the 9th – of January last, until the 1st of the present month.

"The agents appointed by your body, to the United States, to contract a loan and perform the duties of agents generally, have been dispatched and are now actively employed in the discharge of their functions, in conformity with their instructions; and, while at the City of New Orleans, contracted a loan under certain stipulations, which together with their correspondence on that subject, are herewith submitted for your information-- ------------.

"------------ Gen. Houston, Col. John Forbes and Dr. Cameron were commissioned on the part of this government to treat with the Cherokee Indians and their associate bands, in conformity with the Declaration of the Convention in November last, who have performed their labors as far as circumstances would permit, which is also submitted to the consideration of your body. Our naval preparations are in a state of forwardness. The schooners of war, Liberty and Invincible, have been placed under the command of efficient officers and are now on duty, and the schooners of war, Independence and Brutus, are daily expected on our coast from New Orleans, which will fill out our navy as contemplated by law. Our agents have also made arrangements for a steamboat, which may soon be expected, calculated to run between New Orleans and our seaports, and operate as circumstances shall direct. Arrangements have been made by law for the organization of the militia; but, with very few exceptions, returns have not been made as was contemplated, so that the plan resorted to seems to have proved ineffectual.

"The military department has been but partially organized, and for want of means, in a pecuniary point of view, the recruiting service has not progressed to any great extent, nor can it be expected, until that embarrassment can be removed.

THE TEXAS CHEROKEES
1820 – 1839.

"Our volunteer army of the frontier has been kept under continual excitement and thrown into confusion owing to the improvident acts of the General Council by the infringements upon the prerogatives of the Commander-in-chief, by passing resolutions, ordinances, and making appointments, etc., which in their practical effect, were calculated in an eminent degree, to thwart everything like systematic organization in that department---------.

"The offices of auditor and controller of public accountants have some time since been created and filled, but what amount of claims have been passed against the government, I am not advised, as no report has yet been made to my office; but of one thing I am certain, that many claims have been passed for which the government, in justice, should not be bound or chargeable. The General Council has tenaciously held on to a controlling power over these offices, and forced accounts through them contrary to justice and good faith, and for which evil I have never yet been able to find a remedy; and if such a state of things shall be continued long, the public debt will soon be increased to an amount beyond all reasonable conception.

"With a fervent and anxious desire that your deliberations may be fraught with that unity of feeling and harmony of action so desirable and necessary to quiet and settle the disturbed and distracted interests of the country, and that your final conclusions may answer the full expectations of the people at home and abroad.

"I subscribe myself with sentiments of the highest regard and consideration.

Your obedient servant,

Henry Smith

March 1 – 1836.   Governor."

"Executive Department,

Washington,

March 2nd, 1836.

Fellow – Citizens of Texas:

"The enemy are upon us. A strong force surrounds the walls of the Alamo, and threaten the garrison with the sword. A strong force surrounds

29

the walls of the Alamo, and threaten the garrison with the sword. Our country imperiously demands the services of every patriotic arm, and longer to continue in a state of apathy will be criminal. Citizens of Texas, descendants of Washington, awake! Arouse yourselves!

"The question is now to be decided, are we now to continue free men, or bow beneath the rod of military despotism? Shall we, without a struggle, sacrifice our fortunes, our liberties and our lives, or shall we imitate the example of our forefathers and hurl destruction on the hands of our oppressors? The eyes of the world are upon us. All friends of liberty and the rights of men are anxious spectators of our conflict, or are enlisted in our cause. Shall we disappoint their hopes and expectations? No! Let us at once fly to arms, march to the battle-field, meet the foe, and give renewed evidence to the world that the arms of freeman, uplifted in defense of liberty and right, are irresistible. Now is the day and now is the hour, when Texas expects every man to do his duty. Let us show ourselves worthy to be free, and we shall be free.

"Henry Smith,
Governor."

Lacking a quorum, the Council met from day to day only to adjourn. On the 11th, General Thos. J. Rusk of Nacogdoches introduced resolutions in the plenary convention, relieving the Governor and Council of the duties conferred upon them by the Consultation of November 3 – 14, 1835. It now became the duty of the convention to institute a new government.

The convention proceeded with utmost decorum until the 16th when by special enactment a government ad interim was created for the republic until a regular government could be provided for. The ad interim government consisted of a President, Vice President and Cabinet. The President was clothed with all but dictatorial powers. On the 17th, a constitution for the republic was adopted and later submitted to the people for ratification or rejection. The convention elected the first President and Vice President.

The last day of the session fell upon March 18, 1836. The government ad interim elected as officers David G. Burnet, President, and for Vice President Lorenzo de Zavala, the Mexican who espoused the cause of Texas. A full complement of officers was elected, including the re-election of Sam Houston, as Commander-in-chief. The labors of the convention ended on the 18th, and on 21st, moved to Harrisburg. Its members thereupon dispersed. Some joined the army while others made haste to reunite with their families to remove them to places of safety.

30

THE TEXAS CHEROKEES
1820 – 1839.

At the head of the Texas army stationed at Gonzales, General Houston wrote the following letter to Colonel Bowl, Chief of the Cherokee Nation, under date April 13, 1836:

"My Friend Col. Bowl:

I am busy and will only say, how da do, to you! You will get your land as it was promised in our treaty, and you, and all my Red brothers, may rest satisfied that I will always hold you by the hand, and look to you as Brothers and treat you as such!

"You must give my best compliments to my sister, and tell her that I have not worn out the moccasins which she made me; and I hope to see her and you and all my relations, before they are worn out.

"Our army are all well, and in good spirits. In a little fight the other day several of the Mexicans were killed and none of our men hurt. There are not many of the enemy now in the country, and one of our ships took one of the enemy's and took 300 barrels of flour, 250 kegs of powder and much property – and sunk a big warship of the enemy, which had many guns."

The struggle for Texas Independence culminated in the Battle of San Jacinto on April 21st, 1836. With 783 Texans against the army of Mexico, commanded by the President and Dictator, Santa Anna with upwards of 1500 men, General Houston gained a decisive victory, capturing the President and dispersing his army.

While these things were transpiring, the Cherokees were living in quiet and peace on their land in East Texas where they had been domiciled for upwards of seventeen years. True to form, they had placed implicit faith in the Treaty of February 23, 1836. This treaty had been reported to the Provisional Government, as per instructions, on February 29th, 1836, by General Houston and John Forbes the commissioners. On March the 11th, the Governor and Council surrendered all the official documents to the convention. This treaty and report without doubt were among them. If the government did not avail itself of this opportunity to ratify the treaty as was doubtless the purpose of the Consultation, there appears to be no record of it. However, the Texas Government and army were in a precarious state. The former was moved from place to place for convenience as well as for safety, while the army was continually on the march eluding the strong Mexican army, headed by it President, was in pursuit.

The Neutrality, on the part of the Cherokees was sought and obtained at the outset. This was very essential at this stage of affairs, and if it was ever the intention of the government to fail or refuse to ratify the treaty this could not be hazarded at this time.

Under the provisions of the new constitution, the government ad interim passed out of existence. An election was held the first Monday in September, 1836 for the purpose of electing a full set of officers. Sam Houston was chosen the first President of the New Republic, while Mirabeau B. Lamar was elected as Vice President. On October 2nd, they were inducted into office at Columbus, the seat of government.

In December, 1836, the Cherokee Treaty was forwarded to the Senate for consideration, President Houston commenting in part, as follows:

"----------In considering this treaty you will doubtless bear in mind the very great necessity of conciliating the different tribes of Indians who inhabit portions of our country almost in the center of our settlements as well as those who extend along our border."

No action was taken at this session. At the next session a committee was appointed to investigate the report. A report was made October 12, 1837, about ten months after its first submission to the senate. As follows:

"Resolved by the Senate of the Republic of Texas that they disapprove and utterly refuse to ratify the Treaty or any articles thereof, concluded by Sam Houston and John Forbes on the 23rd day of February, 1836, between the Provisional Gov[ernment] of Texas of the one part and the "Head Chiefs", Head Men and warriors of the Cherokees on the other part. Inasmuch as that said treaty was based on false premises that did not exist and that the operation of it would not only be detrimental to the interests of the Republic but would also be a violation of the vested rights of many citizens-----------------".

During his tenure of office as first President, General Houston made no further attempt to secure its ratification by the Senate. That the failure of the Texas Government to ratify rendered it invalid cannot be accepted as just. In summarizing, it will be seen that the provisions for its making were instituted and carried into effect by the Provisional Government. The same was reported to the Governor and Council and lay dormant during the existence of the government ad interim, but was finally resurrected and placed before the Senate in December, 1836. No action was taken until October 12th, 1837, only to be rejected primarily on the grounds that the treaty "was based on premises that did not exist". This took place during the fourth government of the country, while during the first it was necessary, under the then existing conditions, that the Cherokees be treated with and in

THE TEXAS CHEROKEES
1820 – 1839.

the language of Provisional Governor Smith, "the commissioners would go specially instructed, so that no wrong could be committed, etc.-----------". If the premises did not exist" it certainly must have been presumptious[sic] for the government, at its very incipiency, to so assume and act. The "Solemn Declaration" was published to the world by the Consultation unsolicited by the Cherokees.

The treaty commissioners appeared unheralded at the village of Bowles. Houston remarked in his report, "The state of excitement in which the Indians were first found by your Commissioners rendered it impossible to commence negotiations with them, etc.-----------------".

The "Solemn Declaration had been passed, adopted and signed by all of its fifty-four members unsolicited and unbeknown to them. The treaty negotiations were held and concluded on Cherokee soil. That the treaty should have received ratification seems to be the chief argument, especially for the present – day writers to expostulate in endeavoring to justify Texas for the ignominous[sic] expulsion of 1839.

Let us briefly review a few precedents in reference to the non-ratification of treaties by the embryo government of the United States of North America and note their affect.

From the Declaration of Independence until the adoption of the Constitution – from 1776 to 1789 – there was no national administration. Congress had no power to levy taxes, but could simply make requisitions on the states. Congress, therefore, could collect no taxes, could enforce no law against an individual citizen of a state. Our present Constitution was devised to remedy these very defects. It did. It established a National Government to make laws and to execute laws throughout the whole United States. From the years 1770 to 1789 the United States Government ratified nine treaties with the various tribes of Indians, among them the Cherokee. There was no competent authority at the time to ratify them. They were sacredly kept by the contracting parties and no subsequent government ever attempted to review them for either ratification or rejection. The French treaty of 1778 was among those entered into. This meant the success of the American colonies in their struggle for independence. Washington early recognized the necessity of the formation of treaties with the powerful Indian Tribes and so prevailed upon the authorities so to do.

In urging the Council to appoint Commissions to treat with the Cherokees in conformity to the acts of the Consultation, Provisional Governor, Henry Smith said: "I can see no difficulty which can reasonably occur in the appointment of the proper agents on our part, having so many examples and precedents before us. The United States have universally sent their most distinguished military officers, etc.------".

Very little had transpired in the eastern portion of Texas to disturb the tranquility of the Cherokees with the possible exception of Cordova, a Mexican military officer, who attempted to stir up a rebellion against Texan authority. Emissaries Miracle and Flores had been apprehended, and on their persons were found dispatches from Mexico City, to the Cherokee authorities, soliciting their aid in a war to recover Texas. If these dispatches ever reached their destination, there is no record of it. Suffice it to say, if they did, they fell upon deaf ears, because the Cherokees did not attempt to espouse their cause. After a battle with the Kickapoos, General Rusk discovered the dead body of a Cherokee upon the battle-field and complained to Chief Bowles. The Chief answered his attempt to place any blame on his people by pointing out that the individual was a renegade member of his tribe and that whatever his acts, did not render them a national affair.

Notwithstanding, that, under Article Five of the treaty, the Texas Government bound itself "to prevent in future all persons from intruding within the said bounds", and that such treaty was made in conformity to the "Solemn Declaration", members of the Killough and Wilhouse families were alleged to have met death at the hands of unknown persons within the bounds of the Cherokee Nation. Col. Bowles immediately ordered the bodies delivered to the settlements without Cherokee territory, explaining that roving bands of prairie Indians were responsible for the deeds. The efforts of the Mexican representatives to procure the aid of the Cherokees and the murder of members of the Killough and Wilhouse families seem to constitute the entire grounds on the part of the Texas Government to remove them from their homes so long occupied but no legal cognizance was taken of them – long before any Americans touched Texas soil in quest of a home where peace and happiness might be their lot.

She had obligated herself to perfect a survey of Cherokee territory. To carry this into effect, President Houston, in the latter part of 1838, ordered Alexander Horton to make such survey. The south side, which is marked by the San Antonio road, was run, but it does not appear any further effort was made on the part of the government to complete the survey. However, suffice it to say the three remaining sides are natural demarcations, namely – The Angelina, Neches and Trinity rivers.

On October, 27th, 1838, Col. Bowles wrote Horton, which is indicative of his attitude towards Texas, as follows:

THE TEXAS CHEROKEES
1820 – 1839.

"Mr. Horton:

Dear Sir: I have accomplished my desire in raising my men for to guard and aid you while you are running the line. Insomuch I understand that some of the white people are against it, I am sorry to hear that for we wish to do right ourselves and we hoped that white people wanted to do the same. As for your disputes among yourselves, I have ordered my men to have nothing to do with it. My express orders to my men are to guard you and your property from the enemy.

"I hope that you will be particular with us in consequence of us not understanding your tongue and also we will pay that respect to you. I hope you will let us know when you need us and where and I will be at your service.

"I will detain Gayen till I get a line from you as he may read our writing.

I have twenty-five volunteers to send you.

So nothing more,

Only your friend,

Bowl."

Under the wise and able guidance of President Houston, the government under the new republic was a complete success. Order had been restored within her boundaries, the national debt reduced and, in the main, had well taken her place among the sovereign nations of the earth.

Immediately upon the induction of the second administration under President Mirabeau B. Lamar into power, the policy of exterminating all the Indians in Texas was adopted and closely adhered to as will be seen. Lamar had been private secretary to Governor Troupe of Georgia, during whose administration the Cherokees were forced to abandon the homes occupied by them from time immemorial and seek a place of abode in the wilderness west of the Father of Waters. This act of Georgia well places that state in the list of eligibles[sic] for a place in Helen Hunt Jackson's "Century of Shame".

Pretext after pretext was sought in order to find some excuse for the unpardonable sin the government was about to commit upon an innocent people. The act of Cordova appears to have been distorted into the long

THE TEXAS CHEROKEES
1820 – 1839.

wished for pretext. This incident was the chance for the Secretary of War to give vent to his feelings against the Cherokees and to further put into effect the policy of extermination. His letter of April 10, 1838, to Col. Bowl, follows:

"The President grants peace to them but is not deceived. They will be permitted to cultivate undisturbed as long as they manifest by their forbearance from all aggressive acts and their friendly conduct the sincerity of their professions or until Congress shall adopt such measures in reference to them as in their wisdom they may deem proper. With a clear view of all matters connected with their feeling and interests it should not surprise the Cherokees to learn that such measures are in progress under the orders of the President as will render abortive any attempt to again disturb the quiet of the frontier nor it be any cause of alarm to those who intend to act in good faith. All intercourse between the friendly Indians and those at war with Texas must cease. The President directs that you will cause the contents of this communication to be made known to all the chiefs who were present at the council".

A dark and threatening cloud began to gather and envelope the skies. This portended the great and destructive conflagration that was to sweep over the land of the offending Cherokees. Major B.C. Waters, early in April 1839, was ordered to construct a military post on the Great Sabine within the limits of the Cherokee Nation. Col. Bowles mobilized his forces and ordered Major Waters to retire from Cherokee soil, which he did, considering his forces inadequate to cope with his adversaries. This act of Chief Bowles in protecting his domains from intrusion, aroused the ire of President Lamar. He wrote Col. Bowles as follows:

"You assume to be acting under a treaty negotiated at your village on the twenty-third day of February, 1836, with Commissioners appointed by the Provisional Government of Texas"--------------.

He concluded: "I, therefore, feel it my duty as the Chief Magistrate of this Republic, to tell you in plain language of sincerity that the Cherokees will never be permitted to establish a permanent and independent jurisdiction in the limits of this government – that the political and fee simple claims which they set up to our territory now occupied by them will never be allowed – and that they are permitted at present to remain where they are only because this government is looking forward to the time when some peaceable arrangement can be made for removal without the necessity of shedding blood: but that their final removal is contemplated is certain and that it will be

36

friendly negotiating, or by voilence[sic] of war, must depend on the Cherokees themselves."

If the Mexican government desired to place on foot plans for the recovery of Texas is not a matter of speculation or discussion here. Whether or not they desired the assistance of the Cherokees and other tribes of Indians is not material. There is no evidence that these Indians espoused the Mexican cause or made the slightest effort in that direction while on the other hand, indications are that they were heartily in accord with the Texan authorities. If the Texans, Mexicans or other tribes of Indians desired to trade or carry on intercourse, there was nothing in the treaty with Texas, the "Solemn Declaration", or in their own laws or regulations to prevent it. The main point is, did the Cherokee government actually commit any overt acts of war? Then did the attempts of the Mexican emissaries to gain their support in a war against Texas, constitute cause sufficient for the Texan Government to conclude that a state of war existed between the Cherokee Nation and the Republic of Texas?

Let's pause for a monent[sic] and indulge in a retroactive glance into the past. On the first Monday in September, 1838, Mirabeau B. Lamar was elected the second President of the Republic. During the years of 1831-32 when the celebrated cases of the Cherokee Nation vs. Georgia and Worchester vs. Georgia were tried in the Supreme Court of the United States, this same Lamar was private secretary to Governor Troupe of that state. To say that the acts referred to were oppressive and unconscionable is not exaggeration to say the least. Why Lamar left Georgia is not known but on his entrance into Texas, he found a well organized state there, governed by a portion of the same people he knew years before in Georgia, enjoying the confidence of the constituted authorities and wielding a large influence over surrounding tribes. His antipathy towards them must have been well matured and reached the point of over flow. That his policy of the complete extermination of the Indians within Texan borders was well known and "that the boundaries of this Republic shall be marked by the sword" was carried out according to schedule as we shall see. To further the well-established policy of his chief, on May 30th, 1839, the acting Secretary of State addressed the following letter to the Texan Minister at Washington:

THE TEXAS CHEROKEES
1820 – 1839.

"Department of State,

Houston, May 30, 1839.

"Hon. Richard G. Dunlap.

Sir: I am requested by the President to transmit you the accompanying documents, marked as in the subjoined schedule, which were recently captured from a party of Mexicans as you will find detailed in the copy of report of Col. Burleson, Secretary of War, herewith transmitted and marked B2.

"This government has long been in possession of testimony sufficient to justify them in adopting the most summary and imperative measures towards the Cherokees and other bands of northern Indians, resident in Texas. Their unauthorized emigration and protracted stay in our country has always been a source of disquietude and anxiety to the civilized population and their removal has long been desired. But the President, actuated by feelings of humanity towards a people who have been too much accustomed to profit by and abuse similar indulgence, has been unwilling to resort to force to procure their expulsion, while a hope could be entertained that their withdrawal might be effected by peaceable means. That hope has been founded on the application heretofore made to the Government of the United States relative to this interesting subject.. Those applications appear to have been ineffectual thus far, while the humane forbearance on the part of this government toward these intruding Indians, has been productive of many disasters to our frontier settlements, and if longer continued might result in irreparable injury to Texas. The most enduring patience may be exhausted and must yield to the duty of self-preservation, when its exercise evidently gives encouragement and aggravation to the hostile spirit of the offenders. Such is our present condition relative to these immigrant savages; and the President has resolved to put an end to the repeated aggressions of the Cherokees by compelling their departure from our territory. You are at liberty to make known this fact to the government at Washington, and to request that such measures may be seasonably adopted by the government, as will fulfill the provisions of the 33rd article of the treaty entered into between the United States and Mexico on the 5th – of April, 1831, and will effectually prevent the return of these savages to our territory.

"Our right to eject these Indians can scarcely enter into your correspondence with the government of the United States; but should it be incidentally alluded to, you will find it clearly suggested in the letter of Mr.

THE TEXAS CHEROKEES
1820 – 1839.

Forsythe to Mr. Castillo, Charge de Affaires from Mexico which is transcribed in dispatch No. 42 from your predecessor to this department.

"You will not however solicit an elaborate discussion on this subject or any other connected with the obligations of the United States and Mexico; for a protracted discussion is seldom desirable and may be productive of inconvenience, if not of ill-feeling between parties, which we would very sedulously avoid.

"The President conceives that the government of the United States has frankly and justly acknowledged the rights of Texas to the benefits of that treaty, especially in reference to the 33rd- article which has a direct territorial relation to this Republic as now organized; and he cannot imagine that any objection will be raised or difficulty occur on that ground. You will therefore confine your communications, unless constrained to take a wider range, to the fact of the intended expulsion of the Cherokees and such other of the immigrant bands as may proved to have been or may hereafter be implicated in the late atrocious attempt on the part of the Mexican authorities to employ the Indians of the United States in desolating our frontiers. These machinations have been known to us for some time, but are now so fully developed in relation to the Cherokees that longer forbearance towards them is utterly inconsistent with the first duties of this government. If, in the progress of your correspondence it shall be assumed as has been suggested by the Charge de Affairs here, that the government of the United States is not bound to receive or to restrain those Indians and the ill-advised treaty partially made with them on the 23rd- day of February, 1836, by Commissioners appointed by the late Provisional Government of Texas, be alleged in support of this position, you can present conclusive refutation of that assumption in the fact that pretended treaty has never been ratified by any competent authority on the part of Texas. On the contrary, when it was first submitted to the Senate of the Republic which was the only power to confirm it, it was rejected by a decisive vote of that body; and no subsequent action of the government has been had upon it. Indeed should this matter be pressed upon in such terms as to indicate a determination on the part of the government at Washington to avail itself of that treaty, as absolving it from all obligations touching these Indians (which can hardly be possible) you can further disclaim the validity of the treaty on the ground that the provisional Government itself under whose authority the treaty purports to have been made, was acting without the sphere of any legitimate power and could not in any matter so extraneous to the avowed purpose of its creation as the alienation of a large and valuable portion of territory impose any moral or political obligations upon the independence and separate government of Texas. You will recollect that the Provisional Government passed its brief existence anterior to the Declaration of Independence and was organized under the Mexican Federal Constitution of 1824 – that although its organization was in direct voilation[sic] of that Constitution, and may be considered as partially revolutionary, its assumptions of power were no more obligatory upon the independent government of Texas than they would have been on the Federal Government of Mexico had that government been restored and Texas returned to her previous attitude. By the very constitution of that government, Texas, as such, was incompetent to make treaties. She was but a department of the confederate state of Coahuila and Texas, and in her conjunction state capacity was also precluded from entering into treaties with foreign powers. I suggest this as an ultimate plan of argument to be pursued but not to be resorted to except in case of strict necessity. You are aware that the lines designated in the treaty were run by Col. Alex. Horton some time in the fall of the last year at the instance of General Houston, who was then exercising the functions of this government. This fact, too, may be adduced against you; but you will find no great difficulty of diverting it of any serious consideration by suggesting that the act of Col. Horton was without authority, the President having no right to carry a treaty into effect anterior to or independent of the action of the Senate of such treaty. In this instance the assumed right was exercised in direct contradiction to the advice of the senate and every act so done was an absolute nullity, and could impose no legal or moral obligation on this government. Should the government of the United States decline to render you any satisfactory assurance concerning the future return to our territory of the Cherokees now about to be ejected from it, this government will be compelled to resort to its own energies; and a protracted war may ensue between Texas and the northern Indians within her borders. We should greatly depreciate such an event, for it cannot escape an ordinary discernment that it would be more than likely to enlist a portion of the original tribes from whom those intruding bands have been recently removed to the west of the Mississippi by the Government of the United States. It is also more than probable that such a contest would involve the Government of the United States in an Indian war of greater magnitude than any they have heretofore sustained.

"It is not intended to impute error to that government in the congregating of so many[sic] tribes of savages on their remote western frontier, for they did so in the exercise of indisputable right. But while we fully acknowledge the abstract right, we cannot but perceive and deeply regret that its practical operation has been already eminently injurious to Texas and may possibly inflict still more serious evils upon her. The migration of several bands of these very tribes, to our territory was a direct and natural consequence of their removal from their ancient habitations and their location in our vicinity by that government. We entertain too profound a conficence[sic] in the magnanimity of the government of our fatherland to believe for a moment that they still omit to give to this fact all the consideration that an enlightened sense of propriety could suggest; or that they fail to find in it, additional reasons for observance of the treaty of the 5th- of April, 1831, heretofore referred to. No government to act on the beneficient[sic] principles of Christianity will permit itself to prosecute a course of domestic policy, the evident tendency of which is destructive of the peace and happiness of a neighboring nation. It will either abandon the policy or should its continuance be of paramount importance to its own well-being, it will so modify and restrain its pernicious results that the neighboring people may suffer no serious detriment from it. In previous instructions from this government you will find the Coshatties and Buloxies mentioned in connection with the Cherokees and other northern tribes. These bands have been too long residents in Texas (I believe they emigrated from the Creeks during the American Revolution) to be included in the list of intruders from the United States. You will not, therefore, press them upon the attention of that government in your future correspondence. The Cherokees, Kickapoos, Delawares, Pottawottomies, Shawnees and Caddoes[sic] are the bands that have recently entered our territory, and of whom we complain. The Cherokees, Kickapoos and Caddoes are the most numerous and most obnoxious of these, and it is their recall by the United States which we most ardently desire, and to which we are clearly entitled. -------- The President is quiet indisposed, but I trust will be about again in a few days.

Very Respectfully,

I have the honor to be,

Your Obedient Servant,

David G. Burnet,

Acting Secretary of State"

In Order to clarify statements indulged in by the high state officials of the Republic in the foregoing, it is but proper to re—iterate that the first record of Cherokee emigration to Texas was during the winter of 1819-20. The first American, Moses Austin, first saw that country fully ten months after wards, appearing at San Antonio de Bexar, December 23rd, 1820. Before succeeding in perfecting plans to procure empresario contracts for lands on which to make settlements, death over-took him on June 10th, 1821, while enroute home. His dying injunction was that his son, Stephen F. Austin, proceed with the carrying out of his colonization schemes. Under him, the first white or American settlement was made on New Years Creek, in what is now Washington County, January 1, 1822. The Cherokees permanently settled near Nacogdoches about two years before this first American settlement was started.

These "intruding Indian" were hospitably received by the Spanish authorities and were later happily domiciled under the newly instituted Mexican government, which made them full-fledged citizens.

The statements so oft repeated that the Cherokees were "intruders", and their unwarranted long-stay cannot be founded upon facts, if the legal and historical documents of the country can be taken for true. These, founded upon anything other than truth and justice, cannot be successful in hood-winking public opinion in the face of indisputable facts. And the term "savages" may best be disposed of by drawing the mantle of charity over the unsettled conditions of the country; that the Republic was no longer in danger of being molested by her civilized Indians within her borders and the Republic of Mexico. The time was ripe, judging from the trend of events, to dispossess them of the lands to which they had vested rights and repudiate their own "Solemn Declaration" and Treaty.

Much stress has been placed on the 33rd- Article of the Treaty of April 5th, 1831, between the United States of America and the United Mexican States. Just why this seemed to be the logical time and place to do so, is not known. However, for the sake of a comprehensive view of this phase of the situation, article thirty-third is quoted in full, as follows:

"A Treaty of Amity, Commerce and Navigation – Between the United States of America and the United Mexican States :

"Article 33.   It is likewise agreed that the two contracting parties shall, by all the means in their power, maintain peace and harmony among the several Indians nations who inhabit the lands adjacent to the lines and rivers which form the boundaries of the two countries; and the better to attain this object, both parties bind themselves expressly to restrain, by force, all hostilities and incursions on the part of the Indian nations living within their respective boundaries; so that the United States of America will not suffer their Indians to attack the citizens of the United Mexican States, nor Indians inhabiting their territory; nor will the United Mexican States permit the Indians residing within their territories to commit hostilities against the citizens of the United States of America, nor against the Indians residing within the limits of the United States, in any manner whatever.

THE TEXAS CHEROKEES
1820 – 1839.

"And in the event of any person or persons captured by the Indians who inhabit the territory of either of the contracting parties, being or having been carried into the territories of the other, both Governments engage and bind themselves in the most solemn manner to return them to their country as soon as they know of their being within their respective territories, or to deliver them up to the agent or representative of the Government that claims them, giving to each other, reciprocally, timely notice, and the claimant paying the expenses incurred in the transmission and maintenance of such persons, who, in the meantime, shall be treated with the utmost hospitality by the local authorities of the place where they may be. Nor shall it be lawful, under any pretext whatever, for the citizens of either of the contracting parties to purchase or hold captive prisoners made by the Indians inhabiting the territories of the other."

At the time of the formation of this treaty, the Cherokees were peaceably located no their domains. They were full-fledged Mexican citizens and enjoying all the privileges thereto attached. They certainly were subject to the above article so far as the contracting parties, the United States of America and the United Mexican States, were concerned.

But special reference is made in the letter of David G. Burnet, Acting Secretary of State, to the Texan Minister at Washington, bearing date of May 30th, 1839, Texas at that time being a sovereign independent nation. Just how and in what manner would apply to Texas in reference to the Cherokees, has not been pointed out. If it is applicable, it would only have a tendency to force Texas to prevent "all hostilities and incursions" upon the United States, that might have been undertaken by the Indians within her borders. That the heart-rendering desire for the much talked-of "expulsion" that was vividly rising on the horizon of the Lamar Administration, which was later to become a reality and ultimately blacken forever the pages of Texan history, was not touched upon and in no wise contemplates their removal by the 33rd Article. But removal it must be. Texas had so decreed in her might and for what reasons an impartial world and a just Judge of the Universe may yet be the recipients of an acceptable explanation for this murderous and impolitic act.

The following is an account of the Expulsion by Henderson Yoakum. Judge Yoakum was a citizen of Texas, an able lawyer, and in every way a competent judge of all circumstances surrounding the transaction. His "History of Texas" quotes verbatim the account, which is found on pages 263-271- Vol. 11 – 1856.

43

THE TEXAS CHEROKEES
1820 – 1839.

"The treachery of Cordova and the warlike demonstrations of the Indians in Eastern Texas in 1838, are already before the reader, and their causes known. The president in his message of the 21st – of December, 1838, assumed the position that the immigrant Indian tribes had no legal or equitable claim to any portion of the territory included within the limits of Texas; that the Federal government of Mexico neither conceded nor promised them lands or civil rights; that it was not necessary to inquire into the nature and extent of the pledge given to the Cherokees by the Consultation of 1835 and the Treaty of February, 1836, consequent upon it, for the Treaty was never ratified by any competent authority.

Now, the facts are, that in 1822, long before any colonist had settled in Eastern Texas, or any colony contract had been made for that section, the Cherokees immigrated to Texas. They established a village North of Nacogdoches – the town at that time being a waste, lately swept by the forces of Long and Perez. On the 8th- of November of that year, the Cherokees, by Captain Richard Fields and others of their head men, entered into an agreement with the Government of Texas, by which it was stipulated that certain Cherokee chiefs should proceed with their interpreters to Mexico City to treat with Iturbide for settlement of the tribe where it was then located. In the meantime, the agreement guaranteed to the Cherokees the free and peaceful right to cultivate their crops, and the privilege of natives. The chiefs proceeded to Mexico, and the Imperial Government having satisfied them – whether verbally or in writing is immaterial – they returned. An order from the supreme government was dispatched to the Commandant General of the Eastern Providences, and by him to the Governor of Coahuila and Texas, dated August 15, 1831, and by the latter to the Political Chief at Bexar, dated September 1, 1831, directing a compliance with the promise made by the Supreme Government of the Cherokees. The Governor states in his communication that for the preservation of peace with the agricultural tribes he had offered them their settlement on a fixed tract of land, and that they had selected it. He requested the Political Chief to put them in possession, with the prescribed forms. Again, on the 22nd day of March, 1832, Colonel Piedras was commissioned by the Political Chief to put the Cherokee families into individual possession of the lands they possessed. Whether there was an actual written title, is unknown and immaterial. In the empresario[sic] concession afterward made to David G. Burnet, and including part or all of the settlement, the lands already appropriated were excepted from those to be occupied by the colonists under burnet.

For fourteen years the Cherokees had occupied this land, holding it in quiet and undisputed possession. They were not intruders on the whites, for they were the first. The Mexican authorities recognized them as an

44

agricultural tribe, with Mexican privileges and Colonel Bean was official agent for them, in common with other tribes. No voice had been raised against their title. It was deemed by all both legal and equitable. To give weight and dignity to this title, the Consultation of November, 1835, at a time when Texas was weak; when a heavy cloud hung over her hopes and her liberties were suspended upon a most unequal and most unjust war, made a solemn pledge to these Indians, acknowledging their just claim to the lands, setting forth the boundaries thereof, and saying further:

"We solemnly declare that we will guaranty to them the peaceable enjoyment of their rights to their lands, as we do our own. We solemnly declare that all grants, surveys, or locations of lands, within the bounds hereinbefore mentioned, made after the settlement of the said Indians, are, and of right ought to be, utterly null and void."

To make it, if possible, still stronger, the Consultation resolved that each member sign it as a "pledge of the public faith, on the part of the people of Texas", and they did sign it. The names of Wharton, Waller, Martin, Houston, Zavala, Patrick, Henry Smith, Grimes, J.W. Robinson, Mitchell and Millard, among others of the distinguished worthies of the revolution, were placed by themselves to that pledge. Surely they did not intend to deceive the Indians by thus purchasing their neutrality until the war was over, when they, having no further need of them, would declare that the Indians had no title, either legal or equitable. The suggestion that the Consultation had no power to make such pledge is preposterous. The members of it had power to adhere to the Constitution of 1824 or to sever from it; the assembly was organic, primitive, revolutionary. Twenty or thirty thousand people were defending themselves against eight millions. They met, by their representatives, for general consultation. They found a nation of Indians in their midst advanced in civilization and having influence over other tribes. Those Indians had occupied the country first and it was important to conciliate them. This was done by the pledge given. It is a rule in ethics that the promiser[sic] is is bound by what he believed the promise understood by the promise. No mutual reservation or technical objection can avoid this moral conclusion. From all which, the result is that President Lamar's message, in this respect, is unsupported by history, as by the good faith of Texas toward these Indians.

On the other hand, it was impossible that the Indians should have an independent government within that of Texas. They muzf[sic] necessarily come under the Texan laws as citizens. The great object of many was to get their lands, for they were located in a fine and desirable country. The Texans were the first violators of the pledge of 1835. The ink was scarcely dry on the paper when locators and surveyors were soon in their forests; and this, too, notwithstanding the Consultation, by the decree of November 13-1835, had ordered such locations and surveys to cease all over Texas.

"But it in useless to dwell further upon the subject. The Cherokees were charged with the plunder and murder of many of the inhabitants residing among them and in their vicinity. The Killough were cruelly massacred; only three or four escaped, and they were brought into the settlements by the Cherokees, who by their "cunning representations", says the secretary of war, charged these acts upon the prairie Indians, and the treacherous Mexicans. To prevent such occurrences, Major Waters had been ordered with two companies to occupy the Neches Saline, not only to watch the Cherokees, but to cut off their intercourse with the Indians of the prairies. Bowles, the Cherokee Chief, notified Major Waters that he would repel by force such occupation of the Saline. As the Major's force was too small to carry out his orders, he established his post on the west bank of the Neches, out of the Cherokee Territory.

Colonel Burleson, who was then collecting a force on the Colorado to operate against other Indians, was directed to march his troops lower down, so to be ready on the shortest notice to enter the Cherokee territory. In the meantime the government came into possession of the papers of Manual Flores, including those to the Chiefs of the Cherokees. On their reception, Burleson was ordered to increase his force to 400 men and march into the Cherokee Nation. He reached the east bank of the Neches on the 14th day of July and about the same time Colonel Landrum's regiment from Eastern Texas arrived there. The Nacogdoches regiment under General Rusk had arrived some days before and taken position near the Cherokee village. The entire force was placed under the command of Brigadier General Douglas. Commissioners had, for some days, been in conference with the Cherokees to effect, if possible, their peaceful removal. The Commissioners offered to pay them for their improvements, but we have no information that any offer was made for their lands. The Indians were required to surrender their gunlocks and remove to their brethren in Arkansas. At noon, on the 15th of July, all further attempts to make a treaty were abandoned and General Douglas was directed to put his troops in motion. The council ground was about five miles below the Indian camp. When the Texans arrived there, the Cherokees had retreated about seven miles farther up the river. They pursued and a company of spies, which first came in sight of them, was fired on. The Indians deployed their forces on the point of a hill, having a ravine and thicket on the left. General Rusk motioned to them to come on; they advanced and fired

THE TEXAS CHEROKEES
1820 – 1839.

four or five times, and immediately occupied the ravine and thicket on the left. The main body of Texans coming up in the open prairie now formed, and the action became general. The Texans charged the ravine and advanced up from the left. A portion of the Indians, who were attempting to approach the troops on the left flank, were repulsed. The Cherokees fled when the Charge was made, leaving eighteen dead on the ground. The Texans had three killed and five wounded. The engagement commenced a little before sunset and the pursuit ended at night.

On the morning of the 16th, the troops proceeded on the trail made by the Indians the night pervious. In the forenoon, they were found strongly posted in a ravine half a mile from the Neches, and seemed eager for a fight. While the Texan advance was dismounting, the Indians commenced the action, killing several horses and one man before their opponents could form, but they were soon driven by the advance into the ravine. The Indians were protected by a ravine and a thicket in the rear, while the Texans had to advance upon them through an open wood and down a hill. The main body coming up was formed, and firing commenced at a distance of a hundred and fifty yards. The Texans kept advancing and firing until within fifty yards of the ravine, when, upon a signal, they charged. When they reached the ravine, the Indians fled and retreated into the dense thicket and swamp of the Neches bottom. The charge was gallantly continued into the swamp, but the enemy made no stand. Thus ended the conflict of the 16th. It lasted an hour and a half and was well contested by the Indians. The Texans lost five killed and twenty-seven wounded. The loss of the Cherokees was probably a hundred killed and wounded, and among the former was their distinguished Chief Bowles. In the official report of the action he was styled "the long-dreaded Mexican ally, Colonel Bowles". In these two contests there were engaged about five hundred Texans and eight hundred Indians.

The trail of the retreating Cherokees was followed for some days. Several Indians villages were passed, their extensive corn fields cut down and houses burned. On the evening of the 25th, further pursuit being useless, the secretary of war, who accompanied the expedition, directed the troops to be marched to their homes and mustered out of service. "For eighteen months afterward", says a worthy officer in the engagements, "the Indians came back in small parties, and committed fearful depredations upon the lives and property of the people on the frontiers".

In the march of General Douglas, he passed the villages of nearly all the civilized Indians. He says, "the Cherokees, Delawares, Shawnees, Caddos, Kickapoos, Biloxies, and Ouchies had established during the past

THE TEXAS CHEROKEES
1820 – 1839.

spring and summer many villages and cleared and planted extensive fields of corn, beans, peas, etc., preparing evidently for an efficient co-operation with the Mexicans in a war with this country". It was very natural to infer from these agricultural labors, that the Indians were preparing for a war against Texas; but neither their plans nor their crops were permitted to mature. He speaks also of the Indian territory through which he marched and says that "in point of richness of soil and the beauty of situation, water and productions, it would vie with the best portions of Texas".

Thus the vexed question with regard to the civilized Indians was settled, and there could be no hindrance to surveyers[sic] or settlements on their fine lands. The previous administration had endeavored by treaties and presents to conciliate the frontier Indians; this had pursued a sterner policy. It had, in all conflicts, killed about three hundred warriors, leaving five thousand more all exasperated against Texas and ready to unite with her great enemy against her. However, the main point was to secure the lives, property and rights of the Texans; and if that was more thoroughly effected by war, so much the better for the republic. As to the rights of the Indians, much has been said and written in regard to them. Perhaps the excuse offered by Cicero for the extension policy of Rome is the best for us – "that no people have a right to the soil who do not know the use of it."

Following the expulsion, the Cherokee National Council assembled at Fort Gibson, Indian Territory, and took action in reference to the Texas Cherokees as evidenced by the following letter written by M. Arbuckle, Commanding 2nd. W. Division of the United States Army:

"Headquarters, 2nd W. Division

Fort Gibson, April 28th, 1840.

To His Excellency,

Maribeau B. Lamar,

President of Texas

City of Austin.

Sir: I was requested by a Cherokee Council assembled at this Post that the whole of their people now in Texas should immediately return to their nation and thereafter remain in their own country. I have no doubt the

Cherokee people are sincere in the wish they have expressed on the subject; and as many of their people that formerly lived in Texas have returned of late, they hope that the time is not distant when their wishes will be fully accomplished. Under such circumstances they hope your government will not desire to detain any of their people in Texas.

"With respect to the wishes of the Cherokee Nation in relation to some of their people now in Texas, I regard it proper to assure you, that if such of them as may be prisoners, are conveyed out of Texas in the direction of Fort Towson, that the commanding officers of that post will be instructed to issue such quantity of provisions to them as may be necessary to enable them to return to their nation.

"I have the honor to be, sir, with great respect,

Your obedient servant,

M. Arbuckle,

Brevet, Brigr. Gen. U.S.A.

The Texan Secretary of War replied as follows:

"War Department,

City of Austin, 11th, June, 1840.

"Brevt. Brigadier General,

M. Arbuckle, U.S.A.

Sir: You will please accept the thanks of his Excellency, the President, and of this Department for your communication of date Fort Gibson, April 28th – 1840.

"We have suffered and are still suffering most serious injury from the intrusive advances of the Cherokee people, within the limits of our jurisdiction and territory.

"The position in which we stand to the Cherokee people, within our limits is hostile; we should therefore be greatly pleased to see them returned to their legitimate home, and again united with their own people in the United States.

"The Cherokee prisoners have been dispatched to the post most convenient to out command. An attempt to send them to Fort Towson would have been no less hazardous to them than their escort; our prisoners being exclusively women and children.

"We trust that within thirty days from this date they will be at Fort Jessup (La.).

"I have the honor to be, with great respect,

Your obt. Sub.

B. T. Archer,
Secretary of War

By order of His Excellency,

The President."

The following appears on page 146 of the 19th- Annual Report of the Bureau of American Ethnology:

"Those of the Texan Cherokees who did not flee to the Indian Territory drifted into Mexico where some hundred of them are now permanently and prosperously domiciled far south in the neighborhood of Guadalajara and Lake Chapala, communication being still kept up through occasional visits, and attendance at General Councils, with their kinsman in the United States – where the nation has continued since its expulsion from Texas."

When the expulsion took place, General Houston was in the United States on business. On his return to Nacogdoches, he addressed the citizens in reference to same. On his first attempt to do so, he was met with hisses, catcalls and threats of violence. He at last succeeded in gaining an eminence when he proceeded to charge Texas with bad faith on her part and that the expulsion and the killing of the Cherokees on the field of battle was unbecoming a civilized and Christian nation. His commanding figure and eloquence triumphed on this as well as on occasions formerly and afterwards.

THE TEXAS CHEROKEES
1820 – 1839.

President Lamar's Indian Policy attacked.

(Extract from a speech made by Senator Sam Houston, in the United States Senate, January 29-31, 1855)

"I can exemplify to some extent, an impression that I have when I contrast war measures with peace measures. I well remember in 1835, 1836, 1837, and 1838, in Texas, we had peace. The Comanches would come down to the very seaboard in amity and friendship, would repose confidentially in our dwellings, would receive some trifling presents and would return home exulting, unless they were maltreated, or their chiefs received indignities. If they did receive such, they were sure to revisit that section of the country as soon as they went home and fall upon the innocent. For the years I have mentioned, in Texas, we had perfect peace, and, mark you, it did not cost the government over $10,000.00 a year. We had no standing army. A new administration came in and the Congress immediately appropriated $1,500,000.00 for the creation of two regular regiments. Those regiments were raised. What was the consequence? The policy had changed in the inauguration of the president. He announced the extermination of the Indians. He marshaled his forces. He made incursions on a friendly tribe who lived in sight of our settlements where the arts of peace were cultivated and pursued by them - by agriculture and other arts, and by exchange and traffic of such productions of the soil as were convenient. They lived by traffic with Nacogdoches. The declaration was made, and it was announced by the cabinet that they would kill off "Houston's pet Indians". Well, sir, they killed a very few of them, and my honorable colleague (Senator T.J. Rusk) knows very well, if it had not been for the volunteers they would have licked the regular army - and the Indians said: 'I was not there'. The Cherokees had been very friendly and when Texas was in consternation, and the men and women were fugitives from the myrmidons of Santa Anna, who were sweeping over Texas like a simoon[sic], they had aided our people, and given them succor - and this was the recompense. They were driven from their homes and left desolate. They were driven up among the Comanches. What was the consequence? Every Indian on our borders from the Red River to the Rio Grande took the alarm. They learned that exterminasion[sic] was the cry, and hence it was that the flood of invation[sic] came upon our frontiers and drenched them with blood.

"The policy of extermination was pursued and a massacre of sixteen chiefs of San Antonio, who came in amity for a treaty, took place. This was in 1840. Before this army was raised they had been in the habit of coming down for purposes of peace and commerce. But an army of Indians marched

51

through the settlements to the seaboard, one hundred and fifty miles, undetected, I grant you, avoiding the dense settlements, went to Linville upon tidewater, rifled the stores and slaughtered the men. If there were any, the women were treated with cruelty and their children's brains dashed out a against the walls of peaceful habitations. The exterminating policy brought it on. The country became involved in millions of debt, and the Indians were kept in constant irritation. That was in 1840 and it was not until the year 1842 that intercourse could be had with them through the pipe of peace, the wampum and the evidence of friendship".

On page 57, Volume of his History of van Zandt County, Texas, Wentworth Manning says: "After the Cherokees had been driven out of East Texas, the fight opened up for the valuable lands formerly occupied by them. The reason for their expulsion became apparent among the pale faced contestants in a mad scramble of possessing the territory from which they were dispossessed was fierce to the Echo."

On page 549, Volume 1, John Henry Brown's History of Texas, says: "The noble Travis, in command at San Antonio, increased his force to one hundred and fifty men and prepared by every means in his power to defend the place to the last. Governor Smith kept couriers in the saddle dispatching them to the coast, Nacogdoches, San Augustine and elsewhere, with messages urging the people to action. Houston (and Forbes under his instructions) proceeded to treat with the powerful Cherokees and their allies and secure their neutrality – a matter of life and death importance at that hour."

"Page 400 – same Volume, says: "This Solemn Declaration" at a later day, as will be seen hereafter, became the subject of acrimonious disputations, but language could not be made more plain or obligatory than was this guarantee to these tribes."

No better evidence can be adduced as to the circumstances surrounding the Expulsion of 1839, than the testimony of Texan statesmen and writers quoted in the foregoing passages. No shadow of doubt can be cast upon the statements of the immortal Houston, Terrell, Yoakum, Brown and others of that day or of Wentworth Manning of Wills Point, Texas, of today. The government, with its regular and volunteer armies, was present on the battle field. The highest state official to the lowest military officer of the armies were present, directing the operations. No other than the renowned Albert Johnson of later Confederate fame, then the Texan Secretary of War was on the field, as well as the Vice President, David G. Burnet, of the

Republic, acting president, instead of Lamar, who was absent in the United States.

Owing to the agitated state of the country and expecially[sic] in reference to title to the lands so lately left vacant by the well planned and hasty expulsion, General Sam Houston, then serving his second term as President, requested the Attorney General of the Republic for his opinion as to the legality of the title under which the Cherokees occupied their lands. Without doubt one of the ablest documents of the kind over pronounced in America was rendered, as follows:

"Opinion of the Attorney General in reference to the Cherokee lands.

"City of Houston, Sept. 10th, 1842.

To His Excellency, The President,

Sir: ------------ You ask my opinion of the title by which the Cherokee Indians held the lands lately possessed by them in Eastern Texas.

"Deeply impressed with the magnitude of the interest involved, and aware of the deep excitement which pervades the public mind on the subject, I have endeavored to bring to its investigation all the energies of my limited capacity.   The question naturally[sic] divides itself into two branches, corresponding to the two governments under which the claim has grown up. The first of those being the Mexican Government, I shall first dispose of that branch of the subject.

"The Republic of Mexico, by legislative enactments of both her general and state governments, invited the Indian tribes residing within and bordering on her territories, to settle within the limits of the Republic. The Cherokees, availing themselves of this invitation, selected the section of country under consideration for their permanent residence. I have never seen any evidence that they ever obtained a grant for these lands from the government, but there is sufficient evidence of several acts of government authorities, such as the ordering of intruders to be driven off from their lands, and others, which clearly showed that the government recognized their settlement-right to the lands they occupied.   This settlement-right was considered by the Mexican laws as the first or incipient stage of title to the lands thus occupied. They were considered by those laws as appropriated, and no longer subject to entry, location, or settlement, by any other person or community, unless abandoned by their first occupants. The Cherokee Indians

53

had, therefore, by virtue of their settlement and continued occupancy, under the then existing laws of Mexico, acquired an inchoate right to the lands on which they resided, which they alone under those laws had the right to mature into perfect titles.

"Thus stood the affairs of the Indians when the first convention, usually denominated the "Consultation", met at San Felipe, in October, 1835. This convention, by one of the most solemn acts recorded in the journals of its proceedings, declared that the Cherokee Indians had 'derived their just claims to lands included within the boundaries hereinafter mentioned, from the government of Mexico, from whom we have also derived our right to the soil by grant and occupancy'. They moreover solemnly declared, that 'we will guarantee to them peaceable enjoyment of their rights to their lands, as we do our own, and we pledge the public faith for the support of the foregoing declarations.' And, as if to give still more solemnity to act and make it, if possible, of more binding force, all the members of the Convention separately signed this guaranty and 'pledge of the public faith'. It would be different to conceive any manner in which a nation could bind itself under more solemn obligations, or affix to its action a higher moral sanction than is here done. 'The language of the instrument partakes largely of the strong and deep feelings that marked the crisis at which it was put forth'. I cannot well imagine in what manner language could be combined better calculated to produce with those to whom it was addressed, implicit confidence in its truth and sincerity.

"The authority of this body however, to make a grant, has been questioned by some gentlemen for whose opinions I have much respect - but with due deference to those gentlemen, I can discover no solid foundation for such an objection. In the language of a gentleman, (the late lamented and talented John Birdsall, Attorney General of the Republic), whose clear hand and vigorous understanding qualified him well for the investigation and elucidation of subjects of this complicated character, and the Consultation was a primary representation of all the people of Texas in their highest political capacity. They assembled independently of Coahuila, and the political organization which had formerly existed, and by this act became virtually severed and separate from the Mexican. They were the only political authority known to the country for the time being and were therefore necessarily charged with the duties and attributes of Government. They were the government de facto. They exercised the prerogative of government. They suspended laws then in force and closed the courts of justice. They enacted laws and caused them to be executed; and, finally, they organized a provisional government for Texas, independently of the other Mexican states."

"These were the purposes for which this body convened. The constitutional government of 1824, under the mild and salutary influence of which the Anglo American population had been invited into the country, had been overturned, and in its stead a military despotism substituted - and a large armed force sent into the country to reduce the refractory Americans to obedience. In this state of things and for causes, was the convention of 1835 called by 'the people of all Texas'. The deliberations of that body therefore necessarily took a wide range, embracing within its legitimate scope, the general interests of the then Department of the Texas. This was the body which not only recognized the claim of the Cherokee Indians to the lands in question as being derived from the laws of Mexico, but which also guaranteed to them 'the peaceable enjoyment of their rights to their lands', and which guaranty to consultation had, in my opinion, ample authority to make. This convention not only guaranteed to the Indians their right to those lands - but they authorized and required the provisional government, which they organized, to make a treaty with them, and designate their boundaries, which was done in accordance with the authority and instructions given by the provisional government, and consequently binding upon the government and people of the country. Had not this guaranty and pledge of the public faith been made to the Indians by the convention directly, the provisional government would have possessed the authority to grant the lands in question to the Indians. The body was invested by the convention with full powers to conduct the political affairs of the country. They combined in that body the functions of political powers, to-wit: the Legislative and Executive. Hence, it follows, that the convention made any specific grant of these lands to the Indians, the authority of the Provisional Government to do so, would have been fairly deducible from the general powers with which that body was clothed. This body exercised all the attributes and functions of government from November 1835, until sometime in March, 1836; during which time it was the only political authority known to or recognized by the country; consequently, a grant of any portion of the public domain by that body would have been considered void. To admit this fact and to deny the validity of a grant made by the convention which created the Provisional Government, and from which alone it derived its powers, would be a solecism in reasoning. It would be, to make the powers of the creature greater than those of the creator – the authority of the agent superior to that of the principal. Had the Convention, which framed the Constitution granted these lands to the Indians – or had the first Congress that assembled under the constitution[sic] done so, their right would scarcely have been questioned by any person. In my opinion, the grant from the Consultation is equally valid as if made by the last convention. I can discover no difference in the legitimate powers of the two assemblies. They were both primary representatives of 'the people of all Texas' – assembled for the same general purpose – deriving their authority from the same source, to wit, the people, the great fountain head of all political power. They were both organic in their structure – radical in their character – equal in dignity, plenary in their powers, and similar in the great objects of their convocation. I can see no reason, therefore, why the acts of the one should not be considered as binding and obligatory upon the country as those of the other. It has been urged, however, in favor of the acts of the last Convention, that they were submitted to the people, and by them ratified, which gave to the acts of that body an authority and force superior to those of the former. This by no means follows as a necessary consequence. The only act of the last convention, which was submitted to the people for their approval, was the constitution - that being designated as the fundamental, organic law of the land, by which the nation was to be perpetually governed – it was thought proper that it should be submitted to the consideration of the people. I am not prepared to say, however, that this instrument would not have been of equally binding authority without this submission. Moreover there were many and very important acts of this Convention which were not submitted to the people, but which have ever since been recognized as valid by the nation. Even the Declaration of Independence, that great act of National sovereignty which forever severed the bonds of political union between Texas and Mexico, was never submitted to the people. That body organized a government' ad interim, and elected a president and cabinet, and did many other acts, which were never directly ratified by the people; and yet their validity, so far as I have heard, has never been questioned. The true question in all transactions performed by a delegated authority is, not whether the acts of the delegate have been subsequently acknowledged by the primary authority, but whether the delegate has transcended the powers with which he was invested; and if he acted within the scope of authority, without subsequent ratification; and this upon the well established rule of law, that the acts of the agent are binding upon his principal, unless the agent trancend[sic] the powers with which he is clothed.

"Again, it is urged that the Consultation acted under the Constitution of 1824; and there being no authority clothed with power by that instrument to grant lands except the Congress of Mexico, or some of the States, consequently, any grant made by them was null and void. This, in my judgment, is not entirely a fair method of stating the proposition. The consultation could not have been convened under the constitution of '24, because that body expressly declared that General Santa Anna had, 'by force

THE TEXAS CHEROKEES
1820 – 1839.

of arms overthrown the federal constitution of Mexico, and dissolved the social compact which existed between Texas and the other members of the confederacy'. 'That Texas is no longer morally or civilly bound by the compact of union', the constitution of 1824, which they declared to be overthrown, consequently they could not have assembled under that constitution - but, as they themselves declare: 'the people of Texas, availing themselves of their natural rights', convened a general 'Consultation of the people of all Texas', with the avowed purpose of providing for the general welfare of the country and organizing a government for the time being. It is true this convention did not repudiate the constitution of 1824, but they declared it to be overthrown by Santa Anna. They also recognized that instrument as containing the 'Republic principals', in the vindication and maintenance of which Texas had taken up arms; but they nowhere said that it is still in force and that Texas is governed by it.   On the contrary, a very little attention to the history of that body and its proceedings will be sufficient to convince any candid mind that the object of it convocation was to erect a government separate from and independent of the then existing government of Mexico, and to place the country in the best posture of defense to resist encroachment of the government, for they declare they 'hold it to be their right during the disorganization of the federal system, and the reign of despotism to withdraw from the Union - to establish an independent government, etc.' True, they had declared they had taken up arms in defense of the 'Republican principals of the federal constitution of 1824'. Those principals were the enduring principals of a Republican government, which guaranteed to the citizen the right to choose his own representative - which guaranteed to him freedom of speech and freedom of action, and which recognized all political power to reside in the people; these, and such as these, were 'the Republican principals of the constitution of 1824', in defense of which the convention of 1835 declared they had taken up arms. But had they recognized that constitution as still in force and as controlling their actions, they could scarcely have performed a single prominent act which they did. They could not have organized a Provisional Government - they could not have raised an army to oppose the forces of the government of Mexico - for there is no authority for any of these acts to be found in that Constitution. They, therefore, declared that instrument overthrown by the military usurpers who then exercised despotic powers in the Republic of Mexico, and such was the fact - that great character of the rights of the citizens had been overturned by violence, and upon its ruins a central military despotism erected, subversive of those "principals of Republican liberty' secured to the citizens of the republic by that instrument of compact, between the federal and state governments. By this act of usurpation on the part of the federal government, the states were absolved from all further allegiance to the compact of union. They had an inherent and indefeasible right to resist the encroachments of this 'military despotism'.   This Texas did, as an integral portion of the Confederacy; and it is no argument against her rights to say that Coahuila did not unite with her in the measure - for the political bands which had united these two departments into one state had been swerved by the overthrow of the federal constitution and by Coahuila's adhering to those who had usurped the authority of the federal government.   Moreover, a separate state government had been guaranteed to her by the constitution of 1824, and when the time arrived for her to assume this station in the Confederacy, it was denied her. Therefore, she determined to assert her own rights upon her own responsibility. For this purpose was the convention of 1835 called by 'the people of all Texas'. The authority with which the members of that body were clothed emanated directly from the people - the great source of all political power in a Republican government; and although they did not formally declare an independent National government, they certainly did assume a separate political existence. They took upon themselves all the attributes, and exercised all the functions pertaining to the highest political authority of a state or nation - and for the time being there was no other government or authority recognized by the people in the country, and their acts have been sanctioned by the nation from that time to the present.

"If there be any one attribute of government more unquestionable than all others, it is the right to exercise jurisdiction over the public domain of the country. This right of sovereignty over the soil, has from the first institution of government, been exercised by the existing political authority of every country. The Convention of which I am now speaking was, for the time the highest - nay the only political authority recognized in the country. They did exercise this right of sovereignty over the soil of the country - they made sundry grants of land to individuals - these grants have never, within my knowledge been questioned to this day. Why then should this grant to the Cherokee Indians be questioned more than others made by the same body? Their right to these lands was guaranteed by the convention in terms as strong and explicit as language could convey them. From all these considerations, I conclude that the title of the Indians to the lands in question was valid and unimpeachable.

"The subject of the original Indian title to these lands being disposed of, another question growing immediately out of the decision of the other, presents itself for consideration, viz: What locations and surveys made upon those lands prior to the Act of Congress of 1840, directing their survey and sale are to be respected as legal, and consequently exempted from the operation of this law?

THE TEXAS CHEROKEES
1820 – 1839.

"This is a question of equal importance though of much less difficulty of solution than the former. It is a well established principal of legal decision, that lands, when once appropriated according to the existing laws of any country, do not again become vacant or subject to entry or location, without an inquisition of office, except by special legislative enactment. And of such force and authority has this principal been recognized to be, that even an inchoate right to lands legally acquired, but which has not ripened into a grant or other perfect title, cannot be divested, unless by office found, in the mode prescribed by the existing laws of the country.

"The Cherokee Indians had settled in the country, under the invitation of the Mexican Government, and according to the laws then existing had certainly acquired an inchoate right to the lands they occupied. These lands, therefore, could not be legally subject to location while in their possession - nor even after, without a manifest violation of the above well settled rule of laws of either the General or State Governments of Mexico, and that is the provision contained in the 30th - Article of the General Colonization law of Coahuila and Texas, which declares that when settlers may resolve to leave the state and settle themselves in a foreign country - if they do not sell their lands, they shall become 'entirely vacant'. This, however, was in the case of voluntary abandonment. But the Indians did not voluntarily abandon their settlements. On the contrary, they were forcibly driven from their homes and possessions. Therefore, the provision of the colonization law above referred to, cannot apply to their lands. They must come under the general principal of the law that requires an inquest of office before the lands possessed by them could be legally subject to location and appropriation by the citizens of the country. This inquest of office has never been taken - consequently those lands have never, since the Indians were driven from them, been subject to location, either by the laws of Mexico or Texas.

"From the foregoing facts and reasons, I conclude that none of the locations made upon the lands occupied by the Cherokee Indians subsequent to the date of the guaranty made by the Consultation to the Indians in 1835, are valid and legal; and consequently that none made since that date are legally exempt -------- sale Act of Congress approved March 3, 1905 of Congress of February, eighteen hundred and forty.

"All of which is respectfully submitted,

THE TEXAS CHEROKEES
1820 – 1839.

G.W. Terrell,
Attorney General."

The Cherokee Nation was, up to the time of the conclusion of the treaty of February 23, 1836, an integral part of the Republic of Mexico. When Texas threw off the Mexican yoke and inaugurated an independent government under the Convention, termed the Consultation, the Cherokees remained a separate and independent government from Texas and by this "Solemn Declaration" they were so treated.

As has been noted, this body provided for the appointment of Commissioners to negotiate a Treaty with them which was done on February 23 - 1836. By its terms, their allegiance was transferred to Texas whereby they became a quasi-independent nation, subject to and existing under the suzerainity[sic] of that government. Well may their status be defined as enunciated by Chief Justice Marshall of the United States Supreme Court in Cherokee Nation vs. Georgia:

"Meanwhile they are in a state of pupilage. Their relation to the United States resembles that of a ward to his guardian."

The unwarranted expulsion of the Texas-Cherokees is one of the world tragedies. "The EPIC is yet to be written."

THE GOVERNMENT OF MEXICO	Claim of Cherokee Indians
	Dated Sept. 22, 1924
TO	Filed Sept. 26, 1924
	Recorded in Vol. 172, pg. 169-75,
THE CHEROKEE INDIANS	Deed Records, Smith County, Texas.

Claim filed by John M. Taylor, of Claremore, Oklahoma, R.R. No. 1, Attorney before the Interior Department for Cherokee Indian Claimants, to grant of land claimed to have been given to them by treaty with Mexico, which grant includes all of Smith County. This grant is claimed under treaty with Mexico entered into November 8, 1822, as per records of the General Land Office of State of Texas, a copy of which treaty is attached.

HISTORY OF THE CLAIMS OF THE TEXAS CHEROKEES

The Consultation of Texas, on the 13th day of November, 1835, entered into solemn declaration with the Cherokees, to which both parties set their names, setting forth that the Cherokee Indians and their twelve associate bands had derived their just claims from the Government of Mexico, to the land lying north of San Antonio road and the Neches, and West of the

THE TEXAS CHEROKEES
1820 – 1839.

Angelina and Sabine Rivers; that the Governor and council, immediately on its organization should appoint commissioners to treat with the said Indians, and establish a definite boundary of their territory, and secure their confidence and friendship, that they would guarantee to the Indians the peaceful enjoyment of their rights to their lands, that all surveys, grants and locations made within those limits after the settlement with the Indians are, and of right ought to be utterly null and void. (Yoakum P. 64-65).

These were the pledges made by the delegates to all Texas, and in pursuance of them Messrs. Houston and Forbes, on behalf of the Republic of Texas, proceeded to Bowles Village and concluded the Treaty of 23rd of February, 1836. See document submitted by the President on Indian Affairs, November 15, 1928 to the Texas Senate.

In the year 1839, the Texas Forces attacked the Cherokees in their country, and after two severe battles, in which probably two hundred Indians were killed, the Cherokees fled their country, leaving all their effects.

TO HIS EX. THE PRESIDENT OF THE REPUBLIC OF TEXAS.

Sir I have looked into the treaty with the Cherokee Indians and their associate bands together with the documents accompanying the same, and have endeavored to bestow upon them the consideration and reflection which their importance demands.

As far as it was possible for the general consultation to concede and establish the rights of the tribes in question to the territory designated, The Indian Title was guaranteed by that body in their solemn declaration and pledge made on the 13th of Nov. 1835, and severly[sic] signed by all the members of that body. The language of that instrument partakes largely of the strong and deep feeling that marked the crisis at which it was put forth. It would be difficult to combine language in any form better calculated to produce with those to whom it was addressed, implicit and unqualified confidence as to its truth and sincerity.

If it were admitted that the constitution transcended its legitimate powers in executing the Declaration and pledge referred to, still as the Indians could not be presumed to know the limitations, if any, that were imposed upon the authority of that body, the principles of common justice and good faith would seem to require its fulfillment by the people of Texas.

A little attention, however, to the character of that body and the subsequent course of the Government, will, I think, satisfy all that its powers were fully equal to the authority it assumed. This body, consisting of about sixty members, was a radical and primary representation of the people of all Texas in their political capacity.

They assembled independently of Coahuila and the political organization which had formerly existed, and by this act became virtually severed and separated from the Mexican Empire. They were the only political authority known to the country for the time being, and were, therefore, necessarily charged with the duties and attributes of Government.

They were the Government De Facto, they exercised the prerogative of government, they suspended the land laws and caused them to be executed, they levied troops, created civil and military officers, placed the country in a position of defense and finally organized a provincial government.

If there was any one subject more immediately connected with their duties than another, or more clearly within range of their powers, we should infer from the history of that period, it was that of our relations with the Indian bands upon the Northern frontier. Aware of the importance of cultivating a friendly understanding with these Indians, the Mexican Government had in May '35 made provisions for selecting from their vacant lands in Texas such a district as should seem most appropriate for their location.

On the 13th of Nov. following, the Consultation appreciating the policy of such an arrangement, made their Declaration and pledge.

If this was not within the scope of their powers, was the closing of the land offices and the suspension of the land system by them a lawful act. Or if unlawful, are all the titles and surveys made since the offices were ordered to be closed, legal and valid? A little reflection will show us that any attempt to restrain the powers of the Consultation within special limits, and, sustain or invalidate their acts as they seem to fall within or beyond those limits, involves consequences to this country of the most serious character.

In Dec. '35 the provisional Government established by the Consultation on appointed Commissioners to treat with the Indians, in pursuance of the proffer in the Declaration and Pledge, they commissioned them, gave them written instructions and dispatched them on their mission. Their labors resulted in the treaty of 23rd of Feb. 1836.

THE TEXAS CHEROKEES
1820 – 1839.

It will be observed that so far as concerns the claims of the Indians to the District of Country assigned them, as lying "North of the San Antonio Road, the Neches, and West of Angelina and Sabine Rivers", their right is concluded and established by the declaration and Pledge.

To this extent it had become a <u>vested</u> <u>right</u> and the only office of the Commissioners upon this part of the treaty was, to ascertain and fix with more precision, if possible, the <u>bounds</u> <u>and</u> <u>limits</u> <u>of</u> <u>the</u> <u>Grant</u>.

I have compared with some attention the provisions of the treaty with the instructions furnished the Commissioners, and am unable to discern any discrepancies unfavorable to the government.

That it would be more convenient to have all the lands of the Republic clear of Indian Claims, and subject to the disposition of our own citizens, is very plain -- but that they also are of right entitled to a resting (place) and suitable provision in the country where their lot has been cast is equally plain, and whatever may be the disparity between them and us in point of intelligence, power and social condition, they have the same right as ourselves to the benefit of those great principals of natural justice and equity, which are immutable and universal.

I have been favored by Chief Justice Collingsworth with a perusal of the note of his opinion on this subject and fully concur in all the views he presents.

With great respect, Your Obdt. Servt.,

Jno Birdsall,
Atty. Genl.

Copy of Opinion of John Birdsall <u>In</u> <u>Re</u> Cherokee Treaty, from papers in possession of Col. Andrew J. Huston, who says "In a Message to Congress the president quoted this opinion in full "See <u>House</u> <u>Journal</u> Third Texas Congress, 1st Session 87-93. Huston's Message is dated November 19. For the history of this Treaty, see above, this issue of the Quarterly 16-18.

I hereby certify that the foregoing is a true and correct copy of the opinion of John Birdsall, <u>in</u> <u>re</u> Cherokee treaty as found in article by Mrs. Adelia B. Looscan, entitled <u>Life and Service of</u> John Birdsall in the Southwestern Historical Quarterly, Vol. XXVI 44-57

THE TEXAS CHEROKEES
1820 – 1839.

Given under my hand and seal in virtue of the Authority in me vested by articles 256, 3722, 3731 of the revised civil statutes of the State of Texas, adopted at the regular session of the Thirty-ninth Legislature 1925, on this the Eight day of February Nineteen Hundred and Twenty-six in the City of Austin, County of Travis, State of Texas.

Octavia F. Rogan
State Librarian

STATE
SEAL
Library

APPENDIX 1

Guion Miller Cherokee applications (1906-1910) and family communication to show family relationship between Lawyer George Fields, Jr. (1921); his father, George W. Fields; and his grand-father Chief Richard Fields (1819), who emigrated to Texas from Sale Creek, Hamilton County, Tennessee.

Special Commissioner of the Court of Claims,
601 Ouray Building, Washington, D. C.

SIR:

I hereby make application for such share as may be due me of the fund appropriated by the Act of Congress, approved June 30, 1906, in accordance with the decrees of the Court of Claims of May 18, 1905, and May 28, 1906, in favor of the Eastern Cherokees. The evidence of identity is herewith subjoined.

NOTE: Answers to all questions should be short, but complete. If you can not answer, so state.

1. State full name—

    English name: *George Fields, Jr.*

    Indian name: _____

2. Residence and post office: *Ind. Terr. P.O. Southwest City, Mo.*

3. County: _____

4. State: _____

5. How old are you? *Twenty five* Born *July, 10, 1882.*

6. Where were you born? *Cherokee Nation — West*

7. Are you married? *Yes*

8. Name and age of wife or husband: *Lula J. Fields, nee Glass, age 25.*

9. To what tribe of Indians does he or she belong? *Cherokee*

10. Name all your children who were living on May 28, 1906, giving their ages:

	NAME.	AGE.	BORN.
(1)			
(2)			
(3)			
(4)			
(5)			
(6)			

11. Give names of your father and mother, and your mother's name before marriage: _____

    Father—English name: *George Fields*

    Indian name: _____

    Mother—English name: *Sarah Fields*

    Indian name: _____

    Maiden name: *Sarah McGhee*

12. Where were they born?

    Father: *Cherokee Nation — East*

    Mother: *Cherokee Nation — West*

13. Where did they reside in 1851, if living at that time?

Father: _Cherokee Nation — West_

Mother: _Cherokee Nation — West_

14. Date of death of your father and mother:

Father:

Mother:

15. Were they ever enrolled for money, annuities, land or other benefits? If so, state when and where,
and with what tribe of Indians: _Cherokee Nation — West. In all_
except share in Old Settlers' Payment

16. Name all your brothers and sisters, giving ages, and residence if possible:

NAME.	BORN.	DIED.
(1) Susan	Apr. 11, 1872	
Freeman	Jan. 3, 1875	
(2) Tom	May 10, 1878	
James M.	March 15, 1880	
(3) (Myrtle) George	July 10, 1882	
Laura	March 2, 1884	
(4) Samuel	Jan. 28, 1886	
Bertha	Feb. 23, 1888	
(5) Jeff	Dec. 28, 1891	
Minnie	July 12, 1893	
(6) Perry	Nov. 30, 1896	
Ada — died Dec. 20, 1905, age 11 yrs.		

17. State English and Indian names of your grandparents on both father's and mother's side, if possible:

FATHER'S SIDE.	MOTHER'S SIDE.
Ezekiel Fields	Albert McGhee
Mary Fields	Akey Silversmith
	(Cherokee name) Akey

18. Where were they born? _Cherokee Nation — East._

19. Where did they reside in 1851, if living at that time? _Cherokee Nation_
— West.

20. Give names of all their children, and residence, if possible:

(1) Ezekiel Fields — Southwest City, Mo.
(2) Mary Nick — Catale, I.T.
(3) Ruthie Schrimsher (Deceased)
(4) Lila Scoggins (Deceased)
(5) Jane Padgett (Deceased)
(6) George Fields — Southwest City, Mo.
Richard Fields (Deceased)
Martha Muskrat (Deceased)

67

21. Have you ever been enrolled for money, annuities, land or other benefits? If so, state when and

where, and with what tribe of Indians: *With Cherokees - west -*

Since July, 10, 1882 - In all except Old Settlers' Payment -

22. To assist in identification, claimant should give the full English and Indian names, if possible, of

their parents and grandparents back to 1835:_____

_____

_____

_____

REMARKS.

(Under this head the applicant may give any additional facts which will assist in proving his claim.)

Post Office address- Southwest City, Mo.
Residence — Cherokee nation, Indian Territory -
George Fields, Jr
applicant

I solemnly swear that the foregoing statements made by me are true to the best of my knowledge and
belief.

(Signature) *George Fields, Jr*

Subscribed and sworn to before me this *15* day of *July* 1907.

R. Robinson

Notary Public.

My commission expires

June 16 1908.

AFFIDAVIT.

(The following affidavit must be sworn to by two or more witnesses who are well acquainted with the
applicant.)

Personally appeared before me *Thos Holt*

and *J E Brooks*, who, being duly sworn, on oath depose and say

that they are well acquainted with_____

who makes the foregoing application and statements, and have known *him* for *18* years and

2 years, respectively, and know *him* to be the identical person *he* represents

himself to be, and that the statements made by *them* are true, to the best of their

knowledge and belief, and they have no interest whatever in *his* claim.

Witnesses to mark.   Signatures of Witnesses.

_____   *Thos. Holt*

_____   *J. E. Brook*

Subscribed and sworn to before me this *16* day of *July* 1907.

My commission expires

July 16 1908. *Sherman A Robinson*

Notary Public.

NOTE.—Affidavits should be made, whenever practicable, before a notary public, or clerk of the court. If sworn to before an
Indian agent or disbursing agent of the Indian service, it need not be executed before a notary, etc.

No. *1641*.   Action: *Admitted*

Name *George N. Fields* and *8* children. Residence: *Southwest City, Mo.*

Reason: *Uncle of #242. Enrolled as George Fields, Del. 8/25*

No. *1641*

Name *Geo. N. Fields*

With No. *242*

Remarks:

No. *1641*

1691

69

Sir:

I hereby make application for such share as may be due me of the fund appropriated by the Act of Congress approved June 30, 1906, in accordance with the decrees of the Court of Claims of May 18, 1905, and May 28, 1906, in favor of the Eastern Cherokees. The evidence of identity is herewith subjoined.

1. State full name—

    English name: *George W Fields*

    Indian name: *Chicha Klougausu*

2. Residence: *in Delaware District Cherokee Nation*

3. Town and post office: *South west City Missouris*

4. County: *McDonald*

5. State: *Missouri*

6. Date and place of birth: *Born in 1839 in the old Cherokee Nation*

7. By what right do you claim to share? If you claim through more than one relative living in 1851, set forth each claim separately: *Throu My Self George W Fields & my Father Eg Kel Fields & Dilila Scroggin A Sister & Jane pagett A Sister & Richard Fields, Mons Father & Jinnie Buffington My Grand Mother.*

8. Are you married? *Yes Married in the year 18*

9. Name and age of wife or husband *My wife Sarel Fields Born in the year of 18*

10. Give names of your father and mother, and your mother's name before marriage.

    Father—English name: *Eg Kel Fields*

    Indian name: *Segulla Klougausu*

    Mother—English name: *Polly Fields*

    Indian name: *Wyie Klougausu*

    Maiden name: *Polly Sexton*

11. Where were they born?

    Father: *in The Old Cherokee Nation*

    Mother: *in The Old Cherokee Nation*

12. Where did they reside in 1851, if living at that time?

    Father: *Was Not Living at that time*

    Mother: *Lived in Delaware District Cherokee Nation*

13. Date of death of your father and mother—

    Father: *Died in the year 1864* Mother: *Died in the year 1875*

70

14. Were they ever enrolled for annuities, land, or other benefits? If so, state when and

where: I was Enrolled in Delaware Dist Cherokee Nation in 1851 or 52
and My Mother Drew My Money for Me at Fort Gibson in the year 1851 or 52

15. Name all your brothers and sisters, giving ages, and if not living, the date of death:

NAME	BORN	DIED
(1) Delila Scroggin	in the year 1822	moved to California
(2) Jane Meggitt	1825	in the early days, don't know when they are dead or not
(3) Bertha Abinahee	1827	
Richard Fields	1898	1848
(4) Martha Musknut	1834	
Georgia Field	1839	living
(5) Ezkel Fields	1842	"
(6) Mary Ellen Dick	1845	"

16. State English and Indian names of your grandparents on both father's and mother's side, if possible:

FATHER'S SIDE	MOTHER'S SIDE
Richard Fields	Jennie Buffington
Klanassa	Na ma Klawassa

17. Where were they born? in the Old Cherokee Nation

18. Where did they reside in 1851, if living at that time? in Delaware District Cherokee Nation

19. Give names of all their children, and residence, if living; if not living, give dates of deaths:

(1) English name: George Vickboise   Moses Field Died 1855
   Indian name: Chicska Klawyasa   Wa sah Klawyass
   Residence: in Delaware Dist Cher nation   in Del Dist Cherokee Nation

(2) English name: Nancy Blyth   Ibby Wolf Died
   Indian name: Nancy   Cou here
   Residence: in Del Dist Cherokee Nation   in Del Dist Cherokee Nation

(3) English name: Elizabeth Blaggin   Delila Ferguson
   Indian name: Qua tee
   Residence: in Del Dist Cherokee Nation   in Del Dist Cherokee Nation

(4) English name: John Field Died 1846   Lucy Dick Died
   Indian name: Chi va Klawyasa   Ell sa Klawster
   Residence: in Del Dist Cherokee Nation   Young Snake Del Dist Cherokee Nation

(5) English name: Ezkel Field Died 1846
   Indian name: Si ka h Klawyasa
   Residence: in Del Dist Cherokee Nation

20. Have you ever been enrolled for annuities, land, or other benefits? If so, state when and

where: Enrolle in Delaware District Cherokee Nation for some small amounts & I was also Enrolled in the $50 Toll Re nation on voice & enrolled for the sold's pay ment and crew of this ship Money in 1894 and also was Enrolled by the Dawes Commission and they allotted Lands to Me

21. To expedite identification, claimants should give the full English and Indian names, if
    possible, of their paternal and maternal ancestors back to 1835:

....

....

....

....

REMARKS.

(Under this head the applicant may give any additional information that he believes will assist in proving his claims.)

....

....

....

....

NOTE.—Answers should be brief but explicit; the words "Yes," "No," "Unknown," etc., may be used in cases
where applicable. Read the questions carefully.

I solemnly swear that the foregoing statements made by me are true to the best of my
knowledge and belief.

(Signature.) _George W. Fields_ his X mark

Subscribed and sworn to before me this _24"_ day of _Oct_ , 1906.

My commission expires
april 17 19

Jno W Smith
Notary Public.

AFFIDAVIT.

(The following affidavit must be sworn to by two or more witnesses who are well acquainted with the applicant.)

Personally appeared before me _D. E. Havens_ and
A. B. Shields , who, being duly sworn, on oath depose and
say that they are well acquainted with _George W. Fields_ who makes the
foregoing application and statements, and have known _him_ for _30_ years and _35_ years,
respectively, and know _said_ to be the identical person _he_ represents _him_ to be, and
that the statements made by _him_ are true, to the best of their knowledge and belief, and
they have no interest whatever in _his_ claim.

Witness to mark:

Signatures of witnesses.

D. E. Havens

A B Shields

Subscribed and sworn to before me this _24_ day of _Oct_ , 1906.

My commission expires
April 11 19

Jno W Smith
Notary Public.

NOTE.—Affidavits should be made, whenever practicable, before a notary public, clerk of the court, or before
a person having a seal. If sworn to before an Indian agent or disbursing agent of the Indian service, it need not
be executed before a notary, etc.

72

Southwest City, Mo. Nov 6, '07

Hon. Eunion Mills,
Washington,
D.C.

Sir,

I am a member of the Eastern Emmigrant band of Cherokees and would like to have information as to the status of the payment that is going to take place to said class of people, when I ect.

Yours very truly,
George Fields

George Fields, Jr's Application #29479, Nat'l. Arc. Film M1104 Roll 239.
George W. Fields' Application #1641, Nat'l. Arc. Film M1104 Roll 18.

OKLAHOMA
MAR 22
10³⁰ A.M.
1930
OKLA

Mrs. Penelope Allen,

St. Elmo, Tennessee.

Even with as much history as George Fields, Jr. knew about the Texas Cherokee and his family, he still had questions about his heritage. So his curiosities led him to famed Native American researcher and historian, Penelope Allen, from St. Elmo, Tennessee, in hopes of finding out where his grandfather, Richard Fields, lived prior to his Texas emigration. As you see in the letter his family history points out that his father always said that his mother, Mary Sexton, always told him that their home was on the Hiawassee River about eight miles from where it emptied into the Tennessee River. And Fields goes on to mention that judging from this statement they always thought that it would be Hamilton County, Tennessee, or today what is known as Sale Creek, Tennessee.

Box 4 9 8,

Oklahoma City, Oklahoma,

March 21, 1930.

Mrs. Penelope Allen,

St. Elmo, Tennessee.

Dear Madam:

When I saw you at the Capitol several months ago I
intended to return shortly to supply you with the information you
desired and also to learn about my people who came from Hamilton
County, Tenn. I did return in two or three days and you were gone.

I would be more than glad to hear from you with whatever you may conveniently or consistently send about my great grand
father, Richard Fields, or any other members of the family you may
have run across in your research work.

My father was two years old when his parents left that
section in about the year 1838 and from what he told me several
years ago they must have come from Hamilton County. He said his
mother (formerly Mary Sexton, a white woman), always told him
that their home was on Hiawasse River about eight miles above the
point where it emptied into the Tennessee River and judging from
this we always thought that would be in Hamilton County. However, if
you have run across the family name in your historical work touching
that county, this may be correct.

Hoping to hear from you and assuring you that I will be
more than glad to assist you in any way possible, should you want any
more data from here,

I am, very truly yours,
Geo. W. Fields.

G.W.F-R

75

APPENDIX 2

Newspaper articles and transcriptions concerning the Texas Cherokees.

Newspaper article provided courtesy of *The Daily Oklahoman*
June 2, 1912
On the top right of the page the headline states,
"Texas Cherokees May Bring Suit For Vast Sum"

TEXAS CHEROKEE MAY BRING SUIT FOR VAST SUM

Tribe May Yet Recover for Lands Wrested From Them.

SOME TEXAS HISTORY.

Indians well Treated When Needed; After War Were Ousted.

By S. W. Ross.

Tahlequah, Okla., June 1. – The possibility if not probability of a suit being in-augurated against the state of Texas by descendants of the so-called Texas Cherokees, calls attention to one of the most interesting as well as tragic episodes in the career of this branch of the historic Cherokee tribe.

The ancient ancestral land of the Cherokees lays far east of the Mississippi river[sic]. In that rugged and picturesque region now occupied[sic] by the states of Virginia, North Carolina, Tennessee and Georgia they were a mighty race unknown ages before the caravels of Columbus set forth upon the dread wastes of the Atlantic. Long after the period of colonization the Cherokees were content to live in near contact with the white people, some of them never wished to leave their old land, but early in the past century there were some who became seized with a desire to get away from the white settlements and found for themselves an independent nation. As a result several thousands of these people journeyed to what was then Mexican territory, soon to become a part of Texas in consequence of the successful warfare waged by the American settlers.

It was in the year of 1822 that Bowles or The Bowl, Fields and Nicolek, Cherokee chiefs, visited Mexico for the purpose of securing a grant of land for colonization purposes, but they were not altogether successful, as they only received a promise; but at a subsequent period Don Felix Tresplacids entered into an agreement with them and this agreement was confirmed by Don Augustas Iturbide, emperor of Mexico, on April 27, 1823. But the Cherokees were destined to be disappointed in receiving the right to set up their own government on the land granted to them by the emperor of Mexico, for when in 1826 one John Dunn Hunter, agent of the Cherokees, visited Mexico to receive the title to the lands he met with refusal. Mexico, it was stated, was quite ready and willing to receive the Cherokees as colonists, but not as citizens, neither would that government grant them lands to be held in common.

Indians Incensed.

This action greatly incenses the Indians, and the result was that the Indians decided to turn against the Mexicans and ally themselves with the white people, with the distinct understanding that they were to receive title to their lands from the white people in the event they were successful in finally wrestling the lands from the Mexicans. On December 27, 1826, Hunter and Fields, as delegates of the Cherokees, concluded a treaty of amity and friendship with the whites upon the basis of this understanding. But the Mexicans got some of the Cherokees under their influence and under promises of titles to their lands induced Chief Bowles and a number of his followers to turn against his associates and against the Texans. Bowles or The Bowl event went so far as to assassinate or to have assassinated, his associates, Chiefs Hunter and Fields. Eventually Bowles fell in battle and but a few years ago, just before the dissolution of the Cherokee nation in Oklahoma, his sword was presented to the Cherokee nation by one in whose custody it had been placed.

The Cherokees who did not join Chief Bowles and who remained in alliance with the Texans were to be rewarded, for at the "Consultation of Texas," held at San Felipo de Austin, November 13, 1835, the delegated authorities of Texas entered into a solemn declaration with the Cherokees, to which both parties set their names, setting forth that the Cherokee Indians and their associate bands had derived just claims from the Mexican government to the lands lying to the north of the San Antonio road and the Naches, and west of the Angelina and Sabine rivers, that the governor and council immediately upon its organization should appoint commissioners to treat with the said Indians and establish the definite boundary of their territory and secure their confidence and friendship. It was further agreed that the Indians would be guaranteed the peaceable enjoyment of their rights to their lands; that all surveys, grants and limits made within those limits after the settlement of the Indians were, and of right ought to be, utterly null and void.

These were the solemn pledges made by the delegates of all Texas, and in pursuance of them Sam Houston, who had a few years previous lived among the Cherokees west of the Mississippi, and one Forbes, on behalf of the republic of Texas, journeyed to "Bowles' Village," so named in honor of Chief Bowles, and there they concluded the treaty of February 23, 1836.

But the Cherokees were destined soon to experience the turning against them of the Texans, for in the year 1839 the forces of Texas fiercely attacked the Cherokees in their reservation and after two bloody battles, in which many Indians were killed, the Cherokees fled from their country, leaving all their property and effects. The cause for this unexpected assault, according to the historian, was that the white settlers desired the fertile lands of the district ceded to the Cherokees. The settlers, or many of them, as excuse pleaded that the Cherokees had proved treacherous and aided the Mexicans, the action of Bowles and his band being in mind.

History of Acquisition.

In summing up the entire matter the historian remarks: "The facts are these: that in 1822, long before any colonist had settled in eastern Texas or any colony contract had been made for that section, the Cherokees emigrated to Texas. They established a village north of Nacadoches, the town at that time being a waste, lately swept by the forces of Lory and Perez. On November 8 of that year the Cherokees, by Captain Richards[sic] and others of their head men, entered into an agreement with the government of Texas by which it is stipulated that certain Cherokee chiefs should proceed with their interpreter to Mexico to treat with the Emperor Inturbide for the settlement of their tribe where it was then located. In the meantime this agreement guaranteed to the Cherokees the free and peaceful right to cultivate their crops and the privileges of natives. The chiefs proceeded to Mexico and the imperial government having satisfied them – whether verbally or in writing it matters not – they returned. An order from the supreme government was dispatched to the commandant general of the eastern provinces and by him to the governor of Coahuila and Texas, and by the latter to the political chief of Bexar, directing a compliance with the promises made by the supreme government to the Cherokees. The governor states in his communication that for the preservation of peace with the agricultural tribes he had offered them their establishment on a fixed tract of land and they had selected it. He requested the political chief to put them in possession, with corresponding titles. The reply of the political chief was that the matter should be attended to with the prescribed forms.

Were Not Intruders.

"For Fourteen years the Cherokees occupied this land, holding it in quiet and undisputed possession. They were not intruders on the white settlers for they were there first. The Mexican government recognized them as an agricultural tribe, with Mexican privileges, and Colonel Piedras was official agent for them and no voice had been raised against their rights. Their claim was deemed both legal and equitable. To give weight and dignity to their claim, the consultation of November, 1835, at a time when Texas was weak and when a heavy war cloud hung over her hopes, and her liberties were suspended upon a most unequal and unjust war, made a very solemn pledge to those Indians, acknowledging their claim to their lands, setting forth the boundaries thereof and saying further: 'We solemnly declare that we will guarantee to them the peaceable enjoyment of their rights to their lands as we do to our own. We solemnly declare that all grants, surveys, etc., made after the settlement of the Indians are and of right ought to be utterly null and void.' And to make it still stronger, the consultation resolved that each member sign it as a 'pledge of the public faith on the part of the people of Texas.' And it was so signed. The names of Houston, Warton, Zavala, Smith, Mitchell, Grimes and others of the heroes of the revolution were placed to the pledge. Most assuredly they did not intend to deceive the Cherokees by thus purchasing their neutrality until the war was over, when, having no further need of them, they would declare that the Indians had no title either legal or equitable."

Whites Were Treacherous.

Twenty or thirty thousand people were defending themselves against eight millions[sic]. They met by their representatives in a general consultation. They found a nation of Indians in their midst well advanced in civilization and having a good influence over other tribes. The Indians had occupied the country first. It was important to conciliate them. This was done by the pledge mentioned. Of course it was impossible that the Indians should have a nation within a nation – an independent nation within that of Texas. Necessarily they must come under the laws of the Republic of Texas or emigrate. But it was not proposed to them that they come under the laws of Texas, for hardly was the pledge of 1835 signed ere the surveyors entered the Cherokee country and began their work, notwithstanding the consultation of 1835 had ordered that all surveys and location cease throughout Texas. The Cherokees were charged with murdering and plundering the settlers in their vicinity. A massacre of a family by other Indians had occurred and the perpetrators were captured and brought by Cherokees to the white authorities, but the crime was laid upon the Cherokees who, says the Secretary of War, referring to the prisoners, "were brought into the settlements by the Cherokees, who by their cunning representations, charged the acts of violence upon the Prairie Indians and the treacherous Mexicans."

Says a writer of the period: Major Walters marched to the Neches Saline and Col. Burlison came to the same point with his command. The chief of the Cherokees informed Major Walters that he would resist the occupation of the Cherokee country with force. Commissioners had been in conference with the Indians trying to secure their removal. These commissioners offered to pay for their improvements, but not for their lands. They were required to surrender their gun locks and remove to the Territory of Arkansas. The Cherokees refused, and the Texans invaded their country with fire and sword, leaving nothing to tell the sad story of the civilized Cherokees, but the bleaching bones of the dead, and the smoking ruins of their homes. Texas certainly copied from the history of the Alamo and aped Mexican cruelty as near as possible."

The story of the Cherokees in Texas has been admirably treated of[sic] by Captain Marryat, the noted British novelist, and the state of Texas today no doubt numbers among her population some of the descendants of the old Cherokee pioneers, but the greater number of such descendants are not dwelling in the state of Oklahoma. Some of them are in and near Tahlequah, the old Capital, and their interest in the achievements of their forefathers is great.

Claim Involves Millions.

For a number of years plans have been considered to gain from the government of Texas indemnity for the great losses inflicted upon the Cherokee settlers. At times it seemed that efforts would soon be made to secure such indemnity. But vast difficulties were in the way, journeys to the capital of the Mexican Republic would have to be made and the archives of that country thoroughly examined. The archives of Texas would likewise have to be thoroughly inspected and legal talent of a high order engaged. All of this necessarily would mean the expenditure of a large sum of money, and of this the descendants of the Texas Cherokees were not in possession of a sufficient quantity to have the case taken up. Year after year has passed away, but ever and anon the Texas Cherokee case has been revived and talked about and speculations made as to the feasibility of inaugurating a suit against the Lone Star State. At this time it seems that something may yet be done. It is thought that it may be possible to secure the services of a strong firm of lawyers who will take charge of the suit and press it to a conclusion for a share of the proceeds which would amount to millions of dollars. The United States has always claimed guardianship over the Cherokees. Even today, a full-blood Cherokee, though a citizen of the United States, cannot legally dispose of his land without the removal of his restrictions by the government. He cannot sell his land and remove to another state or foreign government without the express permission of the government. And if the Cherokee of today is under such restrictions, certainly the Cherokees of more than seventy-five years ago were under the charge of the government. Consequently, the government of the United States as guardian could become a party to the suit, could defend its wards' interest and appear against the authorities of Texas. Just what will eventually transpire is problematical, but it is looked forward to with interest by those who claim relationship with the pioneer Cherokees of Texas.

Newspaper article provided courtesy of *The Daily Oklahoman*
April 10, 1921
Bottom of page, L to R sixth column over, the headline states,
"Indian Suit Not Approved"

INDIAN SUIT NOT APPROVED

Claremore Man's Action Is Declared Unofficial by Cherokee Chief.

TULSA, Okla., April 9. – Chief Levi Gritts of the Cherokees, whose confirmation is now pending at the white[sic] house[sic], has not sanctioned the suit filed today in the supreme[sic] court[sic] at Washington whereby John M. Taylor of Claremore represented that the Cherokees seek to recover extensive lands in Texas and Oklahoma, nor has the executive committee of the Cherokees approved of the suit, according to a statement made here tonight by S. R. Lewis, member of the committee and legal representative of the tribe.

"Taylor's action is unofficial," said Lewis, "and his suit will not be taken seriously at Washington for this reason. Taylor has at no time been named as official representative of the tribe, and in filing the suit acted without the knowledge or consent of its legally appointed representatives."

Lewis does not believe there is any basis upon which Taylor can legally launch his case. What the Cherokees want, Mr. Lewis said, is payment for the land allotted to Cherokee freedmen – slaves and descendants of slaves of the Cherokees – a grant by the government which the tribe is now trying to have reversed. The Cherokees own no land within the limits of Tulsa, although there is part of the old Cherokee nation northeast of the city, and never owned lands near Oklahoma City – Oklahoma county being in the old Creek nation. The Cherokees never laid claim to lands in the Texas Burkburnett field, Mr. Lewis said.

Newspaper article provided courtesy of *The Daily Oklahoman*
November 15, 1921
Top of page, L to R fifth column over, the headline states,
"Cherokees Ask Claim Reviewed"

CHEROKEES ASK CLAIM REVIEWED

U. S. Supreme Court Takes Under Advisement Suit For Texas Lands.

WASHINGTON, Nov. 14. – The Texas Cherokees and associated tribes asked the supreme[sic] court[sic] Monday to review their claim to more than 1,000,000 acres of land in Texas. The court took the motion under advisement.

LAND VALUED AT $50,000,000.

Title Given During Revolution and Later Repudiated, Historian Says.

With the filing of suit in the United States supreme[sic] court[sic] against the state of Texas for 1,500,000 acres of land and damages alleged to have accrued for dispossession of the Texas Cherokee Indian tribe from the land since 1839 by the republic[sic] of Texas memory of the pledge of Texas when it came into the union, to absorb all suits and claims which should ever after be filed against the republic, is brought to the fore.

The land, now valued at approximately $50,000,000, is claimed by heirs of the Texas Cherokees, a branch of the Cherokee tribe which was not recognized by the United States government when Indian territory[sic] was annexed, as their village lay outside the bounds identified by the treaty of July 8, 1817, by the United States with the Cherokee nation[sic].

Because of the peculiar nature of the litigation, in that it is in effect a suit against a foreign, though deceased, power, the republic[sic] of Texas, permission was granted to file directly with the United States supreme[sic] court[sic].

The original suit of the Cherokees, according to Dr. Emmett Starr of Oklahoma City, the tribe's historian, was filed in the late 1870s. The attorneys prosecuting the case died before the case was closed, and it was thrown out of court for want of prosecutors.

It was revived in new form, however, when on June 15, this year, formal notice was served of Governor Pat Neff of Texas that the heirs of the Texas Cherokees would file suit for recovery of the land November 14, this year. No estimate of the amount of damages accruing is mentioned in the tribe's petition, according to Doctor Starr, who stated such an estimate necessarily must come later.

The land for which suit is being filed covers all of Cherokee and Smith counties, and a part of Rusk, Gregg and Van Zandt counties, according to a map attached to the petition.

Newspaper article provided courtesy of *The Daily Oklahoman*
November 22, 1921
Middle of page, L to R third column over, the headline states,
"Court Rejects Cherokee Suit"

COURT REJECTS CHEROKEE SUIT

Supreme Tribunal Refuses To Hear Claims of Indians To Texas Lands.

WASHINGTON, Nov. 21. – The supreme[sic] court[sic] announced Monday refusal to hear the case brought by Texas Cherokee Indians involving title to more than 1,000,000 acres of land in Texas.

The United States supreme[sic] court[sic] announced that the case was refused to be heard for want of jurisdiction, adding that it does not come within the scope of the court's powers as defined by basic law and precedent.

Newspaper article provided courtesy of *The Daily Oklahoman*
October 4, 1925
Top of page, L to R sixth column over, the headline states,
"Cherokees Pick George Fields"

In this article, "Fields was first retained by this organization when the first organization meeting was held in Oklahoma City, February 14, 1920."

CHEROKEES PICK GEORGE FIELDS

Oklahoma City Attorney To Present Tribal Claim In Texas Court.

CLAREMORE, Oct. 3 –(Special) – George Fields, a Cherokee and an attorney in Oklahoma City, was retained as attorney for the Texas Cherokees in the mater[sic] of their claim against the state of Texas for the recovery of lands in five counties of that state, at a meeting of the Texas Cherokees, held in Claremore Saturday. The total consideration of the suit is said to be several millions of dollars. Fields was first retained by this organization when the first organization meeting was held in Oklahoma City February 14, 1920.

The claim is based upon a treaty grant issued by the Mexican government about 100 years ago to the original Texas Cherokee settlers. The case is practically prepared and will no doubt be given a hearing in the Texas courts during the winter or early spring. Plans to carry the suit to the United States supreme[sic] court[sic] were outlined by the attorney of the organization.

More than 150 heirs of the original settlers were present at the meeting, which adopted a resolution commending Fields for his efforts and soliciting his further aid in the matters.

WORLD of WORDS by Emery Wian

Chief Bowles Is Described As Colorful

New Book Out By Harold Keith

Merriment In Old Song Is Recalled

Story of Indian Leaders Who Helped Aid America

Old Egypt Is Depicted

Photography's Fun, Not a Science

FUNdamentals Of Photography

Newspaper article provided courtesy of *The Daily Oklahoman*
The Sunday Oklahoman October 31, 1971
Top of page, L to R second column, the headline states,
"Chief Bowles Is Described As Colorful"

91

CHIEF BOWLES AND THE TEXAS CHEROKEES by Mary Whatley Clarke, University of Oklahoma Press, $6.95.

The history of the Cherokees driven into Oklahoma possibly is as well-known (by non-Indians) as that of any Indians who migrated to the state.

But little has been reported about the North Carolina Cherokees who were forced to move to east Texas in 1819 – until the author, a Fort Worth, Tex., resident interested in Texas history became intrigued by "Chief Bowles" or "the Bowl."

Her curiosity and research led to this readable book about a colorful, shrewd leader. The book is Volume 113 in the Civilization of the American Indian Series, the outstanding historical series inaugurated by the University of Oklahoma Press.

The series is filling in – with distinction – the wide gaps in American Indian history. – Ivy Cuffey.

APPENDIX 3

Treaty, with transcription, between the Provisional Government of Texas and the Texas Cherokees, signed in Bowles' Village, February 23, 1836.

This Treaty made and established between
Sam Houston, and John Forbes, Com-
missioners, on the part of the Provisional
Government of Texas, of the one part, and
the Cherokees, and their associate Bands
                    of the other part
now residing in Texas ^ – towit Shawwnees,
Delawares, Kickapoos, Quapaws, Choctaws,
Boluxies, Iawanies, Alabamas, Cochatties,
Caddos of the Naches, Tahovcattakes, and
Unatuquous, – By the Head Chiefs, Head
men and Warriors, of the Cherokees, as Elder
Brother and Representative of all the other
Bands, agreeably to their last General
Council. This Treaty is made
conformably to a declaration made by
the last General Consultation, at St.
Felipe, and dated 13th November AD 1835.

Article First.

                    The Parties declare,.
that there shall be a firm and lasting
peace forever, and that a friendly intercourse

                              Shall

shall be preserved, by the people belonging
to both parties. —

Article Second,

It is agreed and declared
that the before named Tribes, or Bands
shall form one community, and that they
shall have and possess the lands, within
the following bounds. Towit. — laying
West of the San. Antonio road, and beginning
on the West, at the point where the said road
crosses the River Angeline, and running
up said River, until it reaches the mouth
of the first large creek, (below the great
Shawanee village) emptying into the said
River from the north east, thence running
with said creek, to its main source, and
from thence, a due north line to the Sabine
River, and with said river West — then
starting where the San. Antonio road crosses
the Angeline river, and with the said road
to the point where it crosses the Nachis river
and

95

shall be preserved, by the people belonging
to both parties. –

Article Second,

       It is agreed and declared
that the before named Tribes, or Bands
shall form one community, and that they
shall have and possess the lands, within
the following bounds. Towit, – laying
West of the San Antonio road, and beginning
on the West, at the point where the said road
crosses the River Angeline, and running
up said river, until[sic] it reaches the mouth
of the first large creek, (below the great
Shawanee Village) emptying into the said
River from the north east, thence running
with said creek, to its main source, and
from thence, a due north line to the Sabine
River, and with said river west – then
starting where the San Antonio road crosses
the Angeline river, and with the said road
to the point where it crosses the Naches river

                                    and

and thence running up the east side of said river, in a North West direction. –

Article, Third,

All Lands granted or settled in good faith previous to the settlement of the Cherokees within the before described bounds, are not injured by this Treaty, but excepted from its operation. – All persons who have once been removed and returned shall be considered as intruders and their settlements, not to respected. –

Article, Fourth.

It is agreed by the parties aforesaid that the several Bands or Tribes named in this Treaty, shall all remove within the limits, or bounds as before described. –

(TX)

Article Fifth

It is agreed and declared, by the parties aforesaid, that the Land, lying and being within the aforesaid limits shall never be Sold or alienated to any person or

and thence running up the east side of said
river, in a North West direction.

Article, Third,

All lands granted or
settled in good faith previous to the
settlement of the Cherokees, within the
before described bounds are not conveyed by
this treaty, but excepted from its operation. –
– all persons who have once been removed
and returned shall be considered as intruders
and their settlements, not be respected.

Article, Fourth,

It is agreed by the parties
aforesaid that the several Bands or Tribes
named in this Treaty, shall all remove within
the limits, or bounds as before described.

Article Fifth

It is agreed and declared, by
the parties aforesaid, that the land, lying
and being within the aforesaid limits shall
never be sold or alienated to any person or

persons, power or Government, whatsoever
else than the Government of Texas, and
the Commissioners on behalf of the Government
of Texas bind themselves, to prevent in
future all persons from intruding within the
said bounds. ___ And it is agreed upon
the part of the Cherokees, for themselves
and their younger Brothers, that no other
tribes or Bands of Indians, whatsoever
shall settle within the limits aforesaid,
but those already named in this Treaty,
and now residing in Texas. ___

Article Sixth ___

        It is declared that no individual
person, member of the Tribes before named,
shall have power to sell, or lease land
to any, person or persons, not a member or
members of this community of Indians,
nor shall any citizen of Texas, be allowed
to lease or buy Land from any Indian or
Indians.

    Article Seventh
                    That the Indians shall
                                be

99

persons, power or Government, whatsoever
else than the Government of Texas, and
the Commissioners on behalf of the Government
of Texas bind themselves, to prevent in
future all persons from intruding within the
said bounds. And it is agreed upon
the part of the Cherokees, for themselves
and their younger Brothers, that no other
tribes or Bands of Indians, whatsoever
shall settle within the limits aforesaid,
but those already named in this Treaty,
and now residing in Texas. –

Article, Sixth

It is declared that no individual
person, member of the Tribes before named,
shall have power to sell, or lease land
to any, person or persons, not a member or
members of this community of Indians,
nor shall any citizen of Texas, be allowed
to lease or buy land from any Indian or
Indians.

Article Seventh,

That the Indians shall

be

be governed by their own Regulations, and
Laws, within their own territory, not contrary
to the Laws of the Government of Texas.
All property stolen from the citizens of
Texas, or from the Indians shall be restored
to the party from whom it was stolen, and
the offender or offenders shall be punished
by the party to whom he or they may belong.

Article, Eighth.

The Government of Texas
shall have power to regulate Trade, and
intercourse, but no Tax shall be laid on
the Trade of the Indians.

Article, Ninth.

The Parties to this Treaty
agree that one or more agencies, shall be
created and at least one agent shall reside,
especially, within the Cherokee Villages whose
duty it shall be to see, that no injustice is
done to them, or other members of the community
of Indians.

Article, Tenth. The Parties, to this Treaty
agree

be governed by their own Regulations, and
Laws, within their own territory, not contrary
to the Laws of the Government of Texas. –
All property stolen from the citizens of
Texas, or from the Indians shall be restored
to the party from whom it was stolen, and
the offender or offenders shall be punished
by the party to whom he or they may belong.

Article, Eighth.

The Government of Texas
shall have power to regulate Trade, and
intercourse, but no Tax shall be laid on
the Trade of the Indians. –

Article, Ninth.

The Parties to this Treaty
agree that one or more agencies, shall be
created and at least one agent shall reside,
specially, within the Cherokee Villages, whose
duty it shall be to see, that no injustice is
done to them, or other members of the community
of Indians. –

Article, Tenth,

The Parties to this Treaty

agree

agree that so soon as Jack Steele and
Samuel Benge, shall abandon their
improvements, without the limits of the
before recited tract of Country, and remove
within the same, that they shall be valued
and paid for by the Government of Texas,
the said Jack Steele and Samuel Benge
having untill the month of November
next succeeding from the date of this
treaty, allowed them to remove within the
limits before described. — And that all
the Lands and improvements now oc=
=cupied by any of the before named
Bands or Tribes, not lying within
the limits before described shall belong
to the Government of Texas, and subject to its disposal.

(TX)

Article Eleventh.

The Parties to this Treaty
agree and stipulate that all the Bands
or Tribes, as before recited (except Steele
and Benge) shall remove within the
before described limits, within Eight
months from the date of this Treaty.
Article

agree that so soon as Jack Steele, and
Samuel Benge, shall abandon their
improvements, without the limits of the
before recited tract of country, and remove
within the same, that they shall be valued
and paid for by the Government of Texas,
the said Jack Steele and Samuel Benge
having untill the month of November
next succeeding from the date of this
treaty, allowed them to remove within the
limits before described. – And that all
the lands and improvements now oc=
=cupied by any of the before named
Bands or Tribes, not lying within
the limits before described shall belong
                    of Texas
to the Government ^ and subject to its disposal.

Article Eleventh.

        The Parties to this Treaty
agree and stipulate that all the Bands
or Tribes, as before recited (except Steele
and Benge) shall remove within the
before described limits, within Eight
months from the date of this Treaty.
                                Article

Article Twelfth

The Parties to this Treaty, agree that nothing herein contained shall effect the relations of the Saline, on the Naches river the settlers in the neighborhood thereof until a General Council of the Several Bands, shall take the place and the pleasure of the Convention of Texas be known.

Article Thirteenth

It is also declared, that all Titles issued to Lands, not agreeable to the declaration of the General Consultation of the People of all Texas, dated the Thirteenth day of November, Eighteen hundred and thirty five, within the before recited limits, are declared void, as well as all orders and surveys made in relation to the same.

DONE at Colonel Bowl's village on the Twenty third day of

105

Article Twelefth

The parties to this Treaty, agree
that nothing herein contained shall effect
the relations of the Saline, on the Naches
nor the settlers in the neighbourhood thereof
until[sic] a General Council of the Several
Bands, shall take place and the pleasure
of the convention of Texas be known.

Article Thirteenth

It is also declared, that all
Titles issued to Lands, not agreeably to the
declaration of the General Consultation of
the People of all Texas, dated the Thirteenth
day of November, Eighteen hundred and
thirty five, within the before recited
limits, are declared void – as well as, all
orders and surveys made in relation to
the same.

Done at Colonel Bowls Village
on the Twenty third day of

Copy of Treaty
"Courtesy of Texas State Library and Archives Commission."

February, Eighteen hundred and thirty six, and the first Year of the Provisional Government of Texas. − . −

Sam Houston

Witness

his
Fox x Fields
mark

Interpreter

John Forbes
his
Colonel x Bowl
mark

Henry Millard

his
Big x Mush
mark

Joseph Durst

his
Samuel x Benge
mark

A. Horton

his
George W. Case   Oaata Oosoota x
mark

Mattias A. Bingham

his
Corn x Tassle
mark

Geo. W. Hockley

his
The x Egg
mark

Secretary of
Commission

his
John x Bowl
mark

Tunnetee   x   his mark

APPENDIX 4
Chief Bowles' letter to Sam Houston, with transcription, August 16, 1836.

Chief Bowles Letter to Sam Houston dated August 16, 1836
"Courtesy of Texas State Library and Archives Commission."

August 16th, 1836

Dear Brother I have had the pleasure
of receiving your letter which is great
satisfaction to us we would have been in
to have seen you long ago if we had of
kew you had of been in nacogdoches but
we dare not to believe what we hear
for if were to listen to half the tales that
we hear we would appear[sic] in an unhappy
situation for we have heard that we must
all be killed right or wrong both by white and
red
our brother Shawnees have given me great
charge not to travel the road for fear being
waylaid and killed also has been stated

[illegible line]

bound and was be put to death
because he was riting and said to be our
friends therefore he was no better than
us But Dear Brother I will not bother
your head with this altho I was a feared
that their[sic] might be some trough
in it but hoping that we will
all have an opportunity of conversing
face to face with you which
the conversation will be of some lenth
So we will closs it to day expecting
to have the honor of us all meeting to
converse with you and yours.

Drawing of Chief Bowles of the Texas Cherokees
"Courtesy of Texas State Library and Archives Commission"

Index

(FIELDS), Captain Richard 4,5
[ILLEGIBLE], Rutha 69
AHUMADA, Colonel Mateo 12
AKEY 65
ALAMAN, Lucas..................... 6
ALLEN
  Mrs Penelope 72,73
  Sam T...................... 18
ARBUCKLE, M 47,48
ARCHER
  B T 18,49
  Dr Branch T 15
  President 15
ARRINGTON, Wm W................ 18
AUGUSTINE...................... 7
AUSTIN...................... 14
  Moses...................... 40
  S F...................... 16
  S R 13
  Stephen F 8,9,12,15,40

BAGS, John 12
BARRETT, D C...................... 18
BASTROP
  Baron de...................... 5
  El Baron de 5
BEAN 14
  Colonel...................... 43
  Peter Ellis...................8,12,14
BENGE, Samuel 23,24,102,106
BEVIL, John 18
BIG MUSH 24,106
BINGHAM
  Mathias A...................... 24
  Mattias A 106
BIRDSALL
  Jno...................... 62
  John...................53,62
BLAGG, Elizabeth...................... 69
BLYTH, Nancy........................... 69
BOWL...................... 34
  Col 35
  Colonel...................24,30,106
  John...................24,106
BOWLES 14,32,60,75,77,91
  Chief ... 33,35,46,76,89,90,106,109
  Col 33,34,35
  Colonel...................14,46

John 2
BOWLS, Colonel 102
BRAVO 6,7
BROOKS, J E...................... 66
BROWN 51
  John Henry 51
BUFFINGTON, Jinnie 68,69
BURLESON
  Col 37
  Colonel 45
BURLISON, Col 78
BURNET, David G 8,14,15,18,
29,40,42,43,51
BURNHAM, Jesse 18
BYROM, John S D...................... 18

CAMERON
  Dr...................... 27
  John 20,21,25
CAPTAIN RICHARDS................. 77
CASE, George W 24,106
CASTANEDO, Franco de 5
CASTILLO
  Manual Iturri...................... 5
  Mr...................... 37
CLARKE, Mary Whatley 90
CLEMENTS, J D...................... 18
COE, Phillip 18
COLLARD, E...................... 18
COLLINGSWORTH, Justice 62
CORDOVA 33,35,42
CORN TASSELL 24
CORN TASSLE 106
CUFFEY, Ivy 90
CUK-TO-KEH 12

DAVIS, Geo W 18
DEXTER, P B 18,19
DICK
  Lucy...................... 69
  Mary 65
  Mary Ellen...................... 69
DILL, James 3
DOUGLAS, General 45,46
DUNLAP, Richard G 37
DURCY, F...................... 9
DURST, Joseph 24,106
DUST, Joseph...................... 11

DYER, C C 18

EDWARDS..........................8,10,14
    B W 12
    Benjamin W 10,11
    Hayden.................................... 12
EVERETT, L H 18

FIELDS...............................7,8,14,75
    Ada.. 65
    Bertha...................................... 65
    Captain Richard 43
    Chief.. 76
    Chief Richard............................ 63
    Ezekiel 65,68
    Ezkel 68,69
    Fox.......................................24,106
    Freeman 65
    Geo W 1,67,72,73
    Geo W, Jr................................. 71
    George.....................65,67,87,88
    George W...............63,67,68,69,70
    George, Jr...................63,64,66,72
    James M 65
    Jeff.. 65
    John.. 69
    Laura.. 65
    Lula J 64
    Mary... 65
    Minnie...................................... 65
    Moses....................................... 69
    Mr 9,10
    Perry.. 65
    Polley 68
    Polley An 69
    Richard..........3,5,6,9,11,12,65,68,
   69,73
    Samuel 65
    Sarah 68
    Susan.. 65
    Tom... 65
FILASOLA 18
FILISOLA, Vincente 8,14,15
FISHER, Wm S............................ 18
FLORES...................................... 33
    Jose 5
    Manual 45
FORBES 51,76

Col John.............................20,27
John 20,21,22,24,25,26,30,
   31,92,106
Mr.. 60
FOREMAN, Delila.........................69
FORSYTHE, Mr..............................37
FUGA, Benj....................................18

GARZA, Don Felipe de la................6
GAYEN..34
GLASS
    George 64
    Lula J 64
    Sarah..64
GRAPP, Francis 9
GRIMES.....................................44,78
    Jesse..18
GRITTS, Chief Levi.......................81

HANKS, Wyatt................................18
HARDIN, A B................................18
HARRIS, Wm P 18
HAVENS, D E................................70
HE-KO-LAKE.................................12
HOCKLEY
    Geo W 106
    George V 24
HODGES, James............................18
HOLT, Thos 66
HORTON
    A..18,24
    Alexander 33
    Col Alex 39
    Mr..34
HOUSTON................32,44,50,51,78
    A..18
    Gen 27
    Genera Sam 51
    General 20,30,31,39,49
    General Sam 26
    Mr..60
    President....................................33,34
    Sam........ 18,19,20,21,22,24,25,26,
   31,76,92,106
    Senator Sam................................49
HOXEY, Asa...................................18
HUBER, Jos A................................12
HUNTER.....................................10,14

Chief 76
John D 11,12
John Dunn 9,75
Mr 8
HUSTON, Col Andrew J 62

IMPERIAL MAJESTY 4
INTURBIDE, Emperor 77
ITURBIDE
    Don Augustas........................... 75
    Emperor 6

JACKSON, Helen Hunt 34
JOHNSON
    Albert.................................... 51
    A E C 18
JONES, R 18

KELLOG, Albert G..................... 18
KILLOUGH............................33,45
KLAU NU SU, Gen na 69
KLAUGASSU
    Chi cia 69
    Se ka le................................... 69
KLAUGASU
    Chicha.................................... 69
    Wa sah 69
KLOUGASSU 69
    Scqulla 68
    Wyia...................................... 68
KUNETAND 4

LAMAR 51
    Maribeau B 47
    Mirabeau B 31,36
    President 35,44,49
    President Mirabeau B............... 34
LANDRUM, Colonel.................... 45
LEFTWICH, Robert....................... 8
LEGON, W B............................. 12
LESTER, J S 18
LETONA, Governor 14
LEWIS
    Mr 81
    S R 81
LONG 2,43
LOOSCAN, Mrs Adelia B 62
LOPEZ...................................... 6

Don Gaspar...............................5
LORY 77

MACOMB, David A 18
MANNING, Wentworth...............51
MARRYAT, Captain....................78
MARSHALL, Justice 59
MARTIN 44
    Wyly......................................18
MAYO
    H B 12
    Harmon B 10,11
MCGHEE
    Albert.....................................65
    Sarah......................................64
MENIFEE, William......................18
MEXIA, Antonio...........................4
MILLARD..................................44
    Henry............................ 18,24,106
MILLER, Guion 71
MIRACLE..................................33
MITCHELL............................ 44,78
    Asa.......................................18
MOORE, John W 18
MUSH 14
MUSKRAT, Martha 65,69

NANCU.....................................69
NEFF, Governor Pat......................81
NEGRETE................................. 6,7
NICOLEK 75

OOSOOTA, Oaata....................... 106
OOZOVTA.................................24

PADGETT, Jane............................65
PAGETT, Jane......................... 68,69
PARKER
    Daniel 18
    Jas W 18
PARMER, Martin..................... 12,18
PATRICK...................................44
    Geo M.....................................18
PEASE, E M............................21,22
PERAMENDI............................ 14
PEREZ.................................2,43,77
PERRY, A G 18
PIEDRAS

Colonel...............................43,77
Colonel Jose de las...................14
Commissioner.........................14
PIERSON, J G V.......................18
PURNELL, John G......................9

QUA TU...............................69

ROBINSON
  J W.................................44
  James W.................16,18,21,22
  S A.................................66
  Sherman A...........................66
ROGAN, Octavia F.....................62
RONQUILLO, Don Ignacio..............5
ROSS, S W............................75
ROYAL, R R...........................18
RUSK
  General..........................33,45
  General Thos J......................29
  Senator T J.........................50

SANTA ANNA....................30,50,56
  General.............................55
  General Lopez de....................16
SAUCEDO, Jose Antonio...............13
SCHRIMSHER, Ruthie..................65
SCOGGINS, Lila.......................65
SCROGEN, Delila......................69
SCROGGIN, Delila.....................68
SEXTON
  Mary.............................72,73
  Polley..............................68
SHIELDS, A B.........................70
SIGLER, Wm N.........................18
SILVERSMITH, Akey...................65
SMITH................................78
  Governor...............19,26,32,51
  Henry.........16,18,19,20,21,22,25,
 28,29,33,44
  Jno W...............................70
  Meriwether W........................18
SPROWL, John.........................12
STARR
  Doctor..............................81
  Dr Emmett...........................81
STEEL, Jack..........................23
STEELE, Jack........................102

STEWART, C B......................21,22
TAYLOR, John M.....................59,81
TCU SA OH LU NU TER...............69
TERAN, General.......................14
TERRELL..............................51
  G W.................................58
THE BOWL......................75,76,90
THE EGG..........................24,106
THOMPSON
  Alex................................18
  B J.................................12
THORN, Frost..........................8
TRAVIS...............................51
TRESPALACIOS..........................6
  Colonel Felix........................6
  Governor.............................5
  Jose Felix.........................4,5
TRESPLACIDS, Don Felix..............75
TROUP, Governor......................34
TUNNETEE............................106
TUNNETOE.............................24
TURQUI, Tong..........................4

VEHLEIN, Joseph......................14
VICTORIA............................6,7
VILLARREAL, Nabor.....................5

WA HERE..............................69
WADE, R T............................70
WALLER...............................44
  Edwin...............................18
WALTERS, Major.......................78
WARTON...............................78
WASHINGTON...........................29
WATERS
  Major............................35,45
  Major B C...........................35
WEST, Claiborne......................18
WHARTON..............................44
  John A..............................18
WHITAKER, Wm.........................18
WILHOUSE.............................33
WILLIAMSON, R M......................18
WILSON, Chas.........................18
WOLF, Ibby...........................69
WOLFE, Antonio........................4
WOOD, Joseph L.......................18

YOAKUM 51,59
    Henderson 42
    Judge 42

ZAVALA 44,78
    Lorenzo de 18,29